Advances in Mental Health and Addiction

SpringerBriefs in Advances in Mental Health and Addiction

Series Editor

Masood Zangeneh, Richmond Hill, Canada

Over the past several decades we have witnessed dramatic shifts in prevailing approaches to mental health and addiction. Significant scientific achievements have led to novel treatment options that impacted the experiences of individuals with mental disorders. In recent years, new perspectives have begun to influence the way we address mental health and substance dependencies, resulting in a greater emphasis on mental health promotion and prevention strategies. Despite these progressions, mental health care systems too often remain stagnant, fragmented, and peripheral.

Masood Zangeneh

Humber College, Woodbridge, Canada

This sub-series provides an opportunity to expand upon cutting-edge research being presented at mental health or addiction related conferences or colloquia around the world. Each 50-125 page volume would be dedicated to a singular event and would provide an opportunity for scholars to present their research and get feedback from other scholars in their field.

Sachin Batra
Editor

Health and Wellness for All: Navigating Pathways to a Better Life

A Comprehensive Guide

Springer

Editor
Sachin Batra
NICMAR University
Pune, Maharashtra, India

ISSN 2948-2224 ISSN 2948-2232 (electronic)
SpringerBriefs in Advances in Mental Health and Addiction
ISSN 2570-3390 ISSN 2570-3404 (electronic)
Advances in Mental Health and Addiction
ISBN 978-3-031-98978-0 ISBN 978-3-031-98979-7 (eBook)
https://doi.org/10.1007/978-3-031-98979-7

This Springer imprint is published by the registered company Springer Nature Switzerland AG
The registered company address is: Gewerbestrasse 11, 6330 Cham, Switzerland

Preface

We are pleased to present this edited volume, *Health and Wellness for All: Navigating Pathways to a Better Life: A Comprehensive Guide*, which brings together a curated collection of research papers and thought pieces presented at the Conference on "Health and Wellness for All" held at NICMAR University, Pune, on February 15, 2025. The conference was generously sponsored by the Indian Council of Social Science Research (ICSSR), New Delhi, under the Special Call for Vision Viksit Bharat @ 2047, an initiative aimed at shaping India's future through scholarly insight and transformative action.

This volume is the outcome of a collective endeavor to interrogate, interpret, and innovate around the pressing concerns of public health and wellness in contemporary India. As we look toward the centenary of India's independence, it is imperative to foster cross-sectoral dialogues and evidence-based policymaking that prioritize inclusive, equitable, and sustainable health systems. The conference created a vibrant platform for academics, practitioners, policymakers, and students to exchange ideas across disciplines: spanning mental health, nutrition, spiritual well-being, emotional resilience, healthcare access, and technological integration.

The chapters in this collection reflect both conceptual depth and practical engagement. Contributors have drawn from empirical investigations, theoretical frameworks, and grassroots interventions to advance an integrated understanding of health and wellness. Together, these contributions emphasize that wellness is not merely the absence of illness, but a dynamic state of physical, emotional, social, and spiritual well-being.

We extend our deepest gratitude to the ICSSR for their continued support and vision. The event was supported by NICMAR University's leadership, including Dr. Sushma S. Kulkarni (Vice Chancellor). We especially acknowledge the efforts of the entire organizing committee for bringing this initiative to life. We also thank all the contributors for their scholarly commitment and the peer reviewers for their valuable feedback.

It is our hope that this volume will contribute meaningfully to ongoing discourses on public health and well-being and inspire future research and policy grounded in the ideals of accessibility, dignity, and collective flourishing.

Pune, India
November, 2025

Sachin Batra

Acknowledgment

We gratefully acknowledge the support of the Indian Council of Social Science Research (ICSSR), New Delhi, India, for sponsoring this initiative under a Special Call for Vision Viksit Bharat @ 2047.

Contents

Meditation and Mindfulness Leading to Health and Healing: A Perspective to Be Explored (M2 to H2) 1
Abhijit P. Bobde, Komal Singh, Hetal N. Bhinde, and Megha Bobde

Theories in Mindfulness Studies: A Narrative Review 15
Brajaballav Kar and Nilamadhab Kar

The Impact of AI-Driven Health & Wellness Programs on Employee Well-being and Organizational Performance: A Mixed-Methods Investigation 35
Elamurugan Balasundaram, Nagaraj Navalgund, P. Aranganathan, Sanjay V. Hanji, and Meghana Shashidhar

Exploring Psychological Distress in Farmers: A Study of the 2023 Yamuna Floods 53
Sidharth Verma, Nitya Srivastava, and Durgesh Tripathi

Sustainable Workplace Wellness Strategies: Bridging the Gap Between Policy and Practice 63
Ronismita Mishra and Shiv Sankar Das

A New Paradigm in Elderly Care: Usage of Artificial Intelligence (AI) and Robots 77
Sohom Banerjee and Souvik Banerjee

Index 93

Meditation and Mindfulness Leading to Health and Healing: A Perspective to Be Explored (M2 to H2)

Abhijit P. Bobde, Komal Singh, Hetal N. Bhinde, and Megha Bobde

1 Introduction

Mindfulness and meditation have gained a lot of attention as transformative practices that enhance mental, emotional, and physical well-being. Ancient practices, which were based on the traditions of Buddhism, have gained a strong footing in modern corporate settings and healthcare institutions because of the scientifically validated benefits. Mindfulness, defined as a non-judgmental awareness of the present moment, and meditation, a practice to develop this awareness, have been shown to reduce stress, enhance focus, and improve emotional regulation (Kabat-Zinn, 1994). In the fast-paced corporate world, where employees often face immense pressure and stress, these practices are increasingly integrated into wellness programs to foster resilience and productivity. Similarly, mindfulness and meditation are becoming integral to holistic healthcare, helping individuals manage chronic conditions and improve overall well-being (Goyal et al., 2014).

Recent statistics further underscore the relevance of mindfulness and meditation. According to the Global Wellness Institute, 33% of large companies have included mindfulness training in employee wellness programs in 2023, which has increased from 19% in 2019. Moreover, the American Psychological Association reveals that 79% of adults reported a decrease in stress levels during 2022 when they engaged in mindfulness activities, and 70% stated an improvement in concentration and

A. P. Bobde (✉) · K. Singh · H. N. Bhinde
Indira School of Business Studies, Pune, Maharashtra, India
e-mail: abhijit.bobde@indiraisbs.ac.in; komal.singh@indiraisbs.ac.in; hetal.bhinde@indiraisbs.edu.in

M. Bobde
Shri Homoeo Clinic, Shop No. B 1, ABC Convenience Centre, Bavdhan, Pune, Maharashtra, India

S. Batra (ed.), *Health and Wellness for All: Navigating Pathways to a Better Life*, Advances in Mental Health and Addiction,
https://doi.org/10.1007/978-3-031-98979-7_1

emotional control. These statistics indicate growth in the consciousness of these techniques as being basic tools for psychosocial issues and professional operations.

This study conducts an investigation with regard to impact on corporate workforce through mindfulness meditation using both quantitative and qualitative approaches. Through the quantitative approach FFMQ and z-test used for two means were applied and measured the impact before and after the intervention has taken place. This results in an enhanced mindfulness level of 28.487 against a pre-test mean of 26.461, thus supporting the conclusion that it had a meaningful effect on respondents' mindfulness. This is supplemented by the result of reliability analysis conducted with Cronbach's alpha of 0.85 and 0.88 for the two test results taken at pre-test and post-test, respectively. Qualitative analysis, with the help of word clouds and treemaps, showed a more detailed insight into the benefits, with themes such as reduced anxiety, improved focus, and enhanced emotional regulation. The findings are similar to those in Goyal et al. (2014), where mindfulness was proved to be an effective intervention to reduce psychological stress and improve overall quality of life.

The research also highlights the holistic nature of mindfulness and meditation. Apart from increasing concentration and lowering stress levels, these activities dealt with wider issues of the physical and emotional realm. People noticed improvements such as better digestion, less bloating, and higher energy levels. Emotional improvement included greater calmness, gratitude, and resilience. Practical routines like visualization, chanting, and mindful eating came to be major ways of infusing mindfulness into everyday life. This integrated approach gives prominence to the multifaceted nature of mindfulness and meditation, hence being adaptable both in professional and health-related areas.

Thus, mindfulness and meditation are far from being fads; they are critical practices that help address the complex challenge of modern life. Their well-documented benefits, supported by robust quantitative and qualitative evidence, make them crucial tools for improving mental, emotional, and physical well-being. Increasingly recognized by organizations and healthcare providers for their value, it can be expected that the incorporation of mindfulness and meditation in wellness programs and treatment plans will become increasingly common, helping to shape a healthier and more resilient society.

2 Literature Review

The meditation and mindfulness practices have drawn a lot of attention and significance due to their prospective to enhance mental and physical health of individuals. The existing body of research has enough evidence to advocate the favorable impact of these practices on stress reduction, emotional balance, and overall well-being of the users. This literature review aims to examine the mechanics, practical applications, and real-world benefits of meditation and mindfulness in healthcare through the existing body of research available on the said perspectives.

Meditation is a way of calming the mind and achieving relaxation. In today's fast-paced life, we all face internal and external stimuli and pressure to perform as much as possible during our days. With meditation we can experience the balance of mind and body and bring ourselves to a point of relaxation. Meditation has become more popular in Western world nowadays, but has roots dating back thousands of years in ancient times in many health care practices. Meditation is taken from Sanskrit word "dhyana" which means contemplation and attention. The word had been derived from Latin "Meditari" which means to engage in contemplation or reflection. Mediation includes various other activities like relaxation, feelings of satisfaction, and well-being apart from breathing exercises, repetition of sounds, observation of thoughts, and a state of self-awareness. Western meditation contrasts greatly from the one linked with traditional Buddhism and Eastern mysticism in that it is mostly secular, practical, and therapeutic. As it is practiced in the West, mediation encompasses a widespread range of techniques that fall under the umbrella of complementary health care, such as yoga, tai chi, qi gong, etc.

Mindfulness, on the hand, is being present in the present moment and not to delve in the past and future moments without being judgmental. It involves being fully present in the moment by paying close attention to each sensory organ and stimulus, including bodily sensations and breathing. Returning to Mindfulness help to feel less stressed in the moments of discomfort and uneasiness.

Mindfulness and meditation's origins can be unearthed in ancient traditions, especially Buddhism, Hinduism, and Taoism, and have evidence of being historically linked to self-awareness and spiritual development. In present day, numerous therapeutic approaches have incorporated mindfulness and meditation practices. Jon Kabat has revolutionized the clinical settings based on meditation by introducing Mindfulness-Based Stress Reduction (MBSR) program in the late 1970s and paved the way for other benefits of mindfulness on health.

There are many traces that meditation and mindfulness practices impact the brain's structure and function through various mechanisms. Research in the area of neuroplasticity exhibited that meditation could change the brain structure in the areas of attention, emotional balance, and memory among the top (Luders et al., 2009). Mindfulness exercises have helped people to control their emotions by becoming conscious of their feelings (Hölzel et al., 2011). There was evidence of reduced stress by lowering the activity of the hypothalamic-pituitary-adrenal (HPA) axis, reported by Pascoe et al. (2017).

Research studies have shown that physical and mental health has been improved by practicing meditation and mindfulness. Memory, attention, and focus have been increased by meditation techniques. Decreased anxiety and depression have been reported by applying mindfulness-based therapies (Hofmann et al., 2010; Zeidan et al., 2010). Mindfulness-based therapies have upheld effective in the treatment of chronic pain (Cherkin et al., 2016). Research studies demonstrate that practicing mindfulness can help improve immunological function by lowering inflammation and advances general health (Davidson et al., 2003). Meditation has been a savior in cardiovascular health through lower blood pressure and improved heart health (Bajaj et al., 2021). Meditation and mindfulness are ever more being included into healthcare environments. Programs such as Mindfulness-Based Cognitive Therapy (MBCT) and MBSR are used to treat several ailments, such as anxiety disorders and chronic pain, depression, PTSD (Post-Traumatic Stress Disorder) along with cancer treatment.

Work performance and psychological workplace health can be improved by mindfulness and meditation-based intervention. Sometimes the results may be demonstrated after 3 months of involvement though the long-term efficacy has yet to be fully established (Ravalier et al., 2016). In times of crisis, like the pandemic brought on by COVID-19, mindfulness and meditation can aid patients, carers, healthcare professionals, and the general public. While mindfulness and meditation come in varied forms, evidence-based practices like mindfulness-based stress reduction (MBSR) are of special relevance. Stress, anxiety, sadness, and pain scores have improved as a result of systematic reviews of these procedures. Conventional meditation and practice of MBSR program for an enhanced period have depicted the functional and structural improvements in their brains (Behan, 2020). Because nurses frequently experience high levels of stress at work, mindfulness-based stress reduction (MBSR) programs have demonstrated notable promise in managing occupational burnout. In practicing nurses, these therapies have been shown to reduce stress, enhance self-compassion and compassion satisfaction, and ameliorate all facets of burnout (Green & Kinchen, 2021). All things considered, mindfulness and meditation techniques provide an inexpensive, advantageous way to promote mental health and well-being across a variety of contexts and demographics. Mediation and mindfulness have revealed positive impacts equally for professionals and students in education sector particularly in Western contexts—including mindfulness-based stress reduction (MBSR) and related therapies (Kim, 2022).

Innovative directions in emotion parameter, cognitive behavioral therapy, mindfulness at work, mindfulness in positive psychology, and the application of mindfulness practice to children and adults were all highlighted by the bibliographic coupling. Contrasted to other forms of literature reviews, study was able to present a more comprehensive and impartial assessment because of the sizeable sample of publications that were examined. Deeper understanding of the intricate and multidisciplinary subject of mindfulness was made possible by combining three bibliometric approaches, which also provided specific recommendations for further study (Bunjak et al., 2022). Meditation: Evidence Map of Systematic Reviews (Schlechta Portella et al., 2021) presented an evidence map of 191 studies having mindfulness as the keyword and evaluated various meditation techniques. Positive impacts and a positive potential of the practice of meditation have been reported by most of the studies under review. Well-being, quality of life, vitality, and mental health have been the main thrust area, which stands out under 5 major areas of health outcomes. Mindful meditation has positive impact on cardiovascular health by dipping sympathetic activation and stimulating a parasympathetic dominant state, as well as by preventing the inflammatory response (Ghaffari, 2019).

Leveraging the mindful meditation in the healing process of patients can be nurtured by using it as a nursing intervention as the nurses are closer to witnessing the mind, body, and spirit of an individual. Healing process can be augmented by encouraging compassion and inner peace while reducing discomfort and stress and helping people to sympathetically observe their own feelings (Ott, 2004). For every outcome, Mindfulness-Based Cognitive Therapy (MBCT) repeatedly produced greater effect sizes as compared to Mindfulness-Based Stress Reduction (MBSR). This study extends testimony that MBPs are coupled to positive health and well-being outcomes in non-clinical samples. These results contribute to the increasing body of research indicating that MBSR and MBCT could be useful strategies for treating mental illness at subclinical levels and could be incorporated in the public mental health agenda (Querstret et al., 2020). An experiment-based study on 51 university students of Spain showed improvements in eating and resting habits. The study documents that mindfulness program could notably contribute to the treatment of addictions and eating disorders, wherein negative emotional conditions and impulsivity are central features of the condition. Female groups have shown better improvements as compared to male counterparts (Soriano-Ayala et al., 2020).

Mindfulness and meditation is quickly winning traction as an important theoretical concept on health improvements and illness prevention. Studies in the field of scientific and clinical research around mindfulness indicated that mindfulness practices have positive impacts on emotional, mental, and behavioral health of individuals and thus improving their well-being. Samples of young people in both clinical and non-clinical interventions have boosted the idea of improvements in mental health through meditation (Black, 2010). A review of literature including 52 papers of empirical and theoretical work concluded that mindfulness practices lead to more positive states of mind, less stress influencing the brain, stress hormones, the immune system, and the autonomic nervous system. It can alter the eating, sleeping, and substance usage in beneficial ways. Inner technology including awareness, attention, acceptance, and harmonial view on life can promote best health of mind, body, and spirit (Greeson, 2009). Meditation and mindfulness are able to improve mental, physical, and emotional health by various techniques, by reducing depression, stress, and anxiety. It also helps boost immunity and improves lifestyle choices (Vasudeva & Vasudeva, 2024).

2.1 Research Gap

Meditation and mindfulness have the potential to notably enhance health and healing by improving emotional regulation, lowering stress, and stimulating overall well-being. However, to standardize procedures and comprehend the long-term effects of these therapies, more research work is needed. There are promising opportunities for patient-centered, holistic care as mindfulness continues to gain traction in the field of health. Notwithstanding the increasing amount of data demonstrating the advantages of mindfulness and meditation for health, there are still restrictions and difficulties. Variability in practice might be challenging to standardize interventions since different types of mindfulness and meditation techniques can produce different outcomes. Even though numerous studies show immediate advantages, more investigation is required to fully comprehend the techniques for immediate and long-term effects. More experimental research would be needed considering the application of meditation and mindfulness techniques to lead to health and healing during clinical experiences.

3 Research Methodology

This study employs a descriptive and mixed-methods approach to examine the impact of mindfulness and meditation on health and healing in two different groups: corporate employees and homeopathy patients. A mixed-methods design is chosen because it can integrate the rigor of quantitative data with the depth of qualitative insights to provide a holistic understanding of the research questions.

3.1 Sampling Plan

It will include 200 corporate employees taking part in MDPs, as well as 20 homeopathy patients who engage in mindfulness and meditation practices. Stratified random sampling is done for corporate employees to ensure fair representation across the departments, whereas purposive sampling is applied on homeopathy patients who are engaged in mindfulness activities. The small sample size for homeopathy patients will be applied to get the focused, in-depth analysis of individual experiences.

3.2 Research Objectives

Aims of the study are

- To find how mindfulness and meditation influence the five facets of mindfulness among corporate employees.
- To study the role that mindfulness and meditation play in homeopathy patients' health and healing processes.

3.3 Hypotheses

- H1: Practices of mindfulness and meditation greatly help improve the five facets of mindfulness among corporate employees.

- H2: Practices of mindfulness and meditation greatly help to heal and get back (heal) homeopathy patients.

3.4 Sources of Data

Primary data are collected through the Five Facet Mindfulness Questionnaire (FFMQ) for corporate employees and in-depth interviews with both groups to capture their subjective experiences. Secondary data are sourced from academic journals, books, and articles to provide context and support the findings.

3.5 Methods of Analysis

The quantitative data from the FFMQ are analyzed using the z-test: Two Sample for Means in SPSS, which was selected because it is efficient in comparing pre- and post-intervention results. Qualitative data from interviews are analyzed using NVIVO, which enables thematic analysis and identification of patterns that enhance understanding of personal narratives.

This methodology, with an integration of both quantitative and qualitative approaches, ensures a holistic approach to the evaluation of dual effects in mindfulness and meditation across professional and medical contexts.

4 Results

Mindfulness and meditation have been proven to be the most powerful practices in corporate settings, enhancing the mental and emotional well-being of employees, especially in a high-pressure corporate workplace. This research evaluates the effects of such practices on the five facets of mindfulness among corporate employees by applying both reliability analysis and a z-test for two sample means. The findings (see Table 1) underline how much better levels of mindfulness remain post-intervention, highlighting the significance of mindfulness and meditation in improving an employee's attention, consciousness, and regulation (Table 2).

Table 1 Reliability table for pre-test and post-test

Metric	Value
Cronbach's alpha (pre-test)	0.85
Cronbach's alpha (post-test)	0.88
Number of items	39.0

Source: (Data analysis)

Table 2 z-Test: Two sample for means

	Pre-test	Post-test
Mean	26.461	28.487
Known variance	31.94	32.58
Observations	200	200
Hypothesized mean difference	0	
z	−3.5670	
P(Z < =z) one-tail	0.0001	
z critical one-tail	1.6448	
P(Z < =z) two-tail	0.0003	
z critical two-tail	1.9599	

Source: (Data analysis)

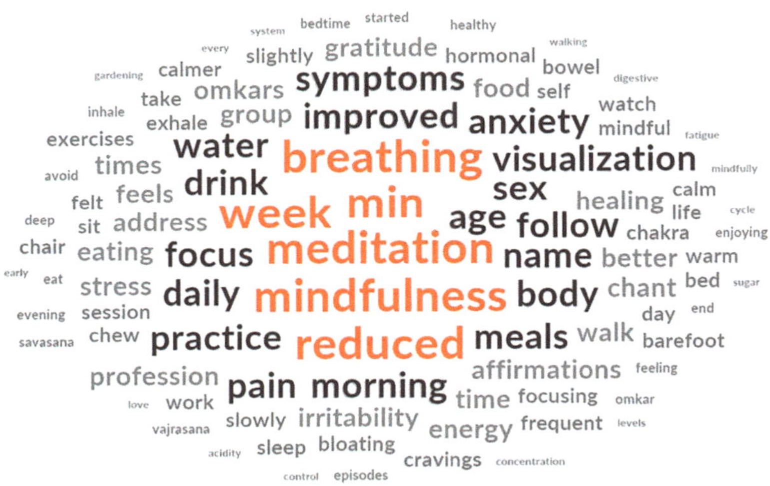

Fig. 1 Word map. Source: (NVIVO)

The z-test of two sample means is used for assessing the five facets of mindfulness among corporate employees in terms of the impact caused by mindfulness and meditation practices. The pre-test mean is found to be 26.461, and the post-test mean stands at 28.487. From the results of the two-tailed p-value = 0.00036 and z = −3.57, which is highly significant at the level of 0.05, this rejects the null hypothesis. This supports the alternative hypothesis (H1) that mindfulness and meditation practices significantly improve mindfulness levels. The observed improvement underscores the effectiveness of these practices in enhancing focus, awareness, and emotional regulation, demonstrating their value in corporate well-being programs.

Qualitative analysis goes deeper into the transformative nature of mindfulness and meditation practices. Visual tools such as word clouds, treemaps, and 3D bubble charts (see Fig. 1) highlight the repetition of core themes—breathing, mindfulness, and meditation—as vital components of health and healing. Key findings from

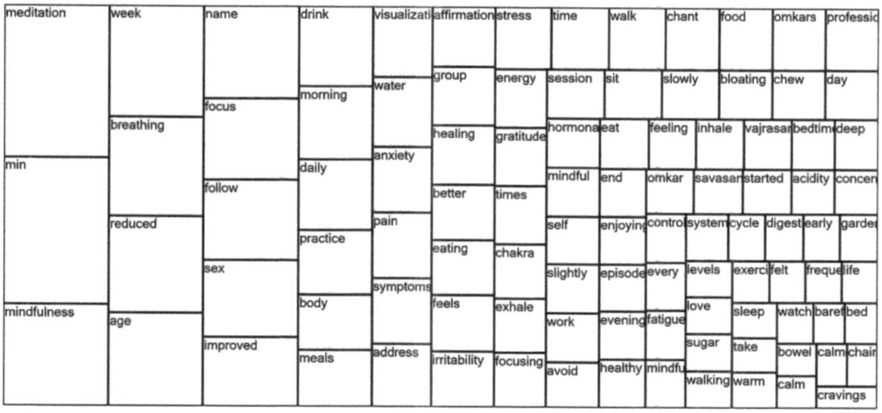

Fig. 2 Treemap. Source: (NVIVO)

analyses are significant decreases in anxiety, pain, and irritation; increases in focus and emotional regulation and general well-being. The inclusion of practical routines such as visualization, chanting, and mindful eating, in addition to emotional elements like calm and gratitude, underscores a holistic approach, integrating mindfulness into daily life for comprehensive mental, emotional, and physical health improvements (Fig. 1).

The word cloud would highlight the themes of mindfulness and meditation. In this regard, the most repeated words would include breathing, mindfulness, and meditation, underlining their centrality in health and healing. It would be very important to see the reduced levels of anxiety, pain, and irritability with improved focus, emotional regulation, and general well-being. Practical aspects, including routine practices, such as daily, morning, or weekly practice, and techniques like visualization, chanting, and mindful eating, are also reflected. References to symptoms, energy, and hormonal changes underscore the physical benefits, while words such as gratitude and calm speak to emotional gains. This represents a holistic approach where mindfulness is woven into daily routines for overall health improvement (Fig. 2).

Treemap highlights key concepts associated with mindfulness and meditation, focusing much on terms such as meditation, mindfulness, and breathing, all indicating their centrality in improving health and wellness. Common benefits usually include reduced anxiety and stress, lesser irritability. Some even mention related physical improvements: better digestion, lighter bloating, and higher energy, among others. It includes practical aspects like daily practice, affirmations, and mindful eating, along with routines such as walking and breathing exercises. Emotional benefits like gratitude, calm, and better focus are also highlighted, showing a holistic approach to integrating mindfulness into daily life for mental, emotional, and physical health (Fig. 3).

The 3D bubble chart represents the frequency and importance of terms regarding mindfulness and meditation practices, where larger bubbles mean more important concepts. Key terms such as mindfulness, meditation, and breathing are emphasized

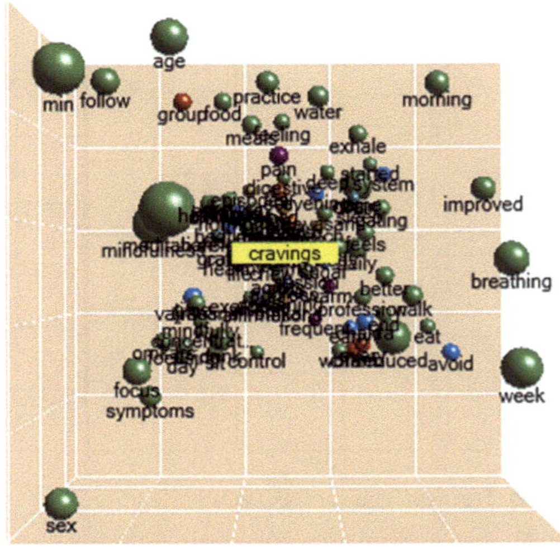

Fig. 3 Cluster analysis using 3D bubble charts. Source: (NVIVO)

as the core of health and well-being. Words such as focus, morning, improved, and practice emphasize routine and tangible benefits, while symptoms, stress, and irritability indicate the challenges these practices overcome. Finally, it also has emotional aspects like calm and gratitude. Thus, this visualization takes on a wide approach, showing that mindfulness is integrated into one's life to help in facing mental and physical health issues.

5 Discussion

5.1 Quantitative Analysis

The results of this study are important findings about the impact of mindfulness and meditation on employees working in the corporate world, specifically about how these practices may be useful for the betterment of their mental and emotional states. The results of the z-test for two sample means reveal a marked improvement in mindfulness levels post-intervention. The pre-test mean is 26.461 and the post-test mean is 28.487. The overwhelmingly significant p-value is 0.00036, thus totally supporting the alternative hypothesis that mindfulness and meditation practices effectively enhance the five facets of mindfulness. Such improvement makes these practices totally invaluable to high-pressure corporate environments by improving how well people focus, are aware, and manage their emotions.

The reliability analysis confirms the reliability of the used measures, and its Cronbach's alpha value shows 0.85 for the pre-test and 0.88 for the post-test, meaning that there are consistent and strong measures for employees' mindfulness level assessment. Findings prove that the Five Facet Mindfulness Questionnaire is valid in determining levels of mindfulness.

5.2 *Quantitative Analysis*

Through the word cloud, tree map, and 3D bubble charts, some repeated themes were detected for further enrichment. Prominent themes are breathing, meditation, and mindfulness, all focusing on the main role of creating health and healing. Emotional and physical benefits, like reduced anxiety, pain, and irritability, and increased focus and gratitude, reflect a holistic approach to well-being. The practical routines like mindful eating, visualization, and chanting further reveal how mindfulness can be incorporated easily into daily life.

These findings altogether point out how mindfulness and meditation practices help toward mental clarity and emotional stability to enhance well-being, making it more relevant for inclusion in work wellness programs.

6 Conclusion

This study aimed at investigating the influence of mindfulness and meditation practices on the five facets of mindfulness in corporate employees. The study had objectives to examine the effectiveness of these practices on improving focus, awareness, emotional regulation, and overall well-being. The quantitative and qualitative study provides robust evidence to support the hypothesis that mindfulness and meditation do indeed significantly enhance mindfulness levels and contribute to mental and emotional well-being in a high-pressure corporate environment.

With a z-test on two sample means, the findings from the analysis are that after the intervention period, mindfulness increased significantly. Improvements were noticeable as shown through the pre-test mean of 26.461 and post-test mean of 28.487. This demonstrates that improvements exist and is confirmed with a very highly significant p-value of 0.00036. Thereby, proving the rejection of the null hypothesis, the result sustains the alternative hypothesis, (H1). Reliability analysis further validated the findings. The Cronbach's alpha values were 0.85 and 0.88 for the pre-test and post-test, respectively, indicating that the facets of mindfulness had good consistency and robustness in their measurement.

Acknowledgments The author expresses sincere gratitude to all participants for their valuable contributions to this research and to the organization for supporting the study. Special thanks are extended to mentors and colleagues for their guidance and to the research team for their unwavering assistance throughout the project.

References

Bajaj, B., Gupta, R., & Pande, N. (2021). The effects of meditation on cardiovascular health. *Journal of Mind-Body Medicine, 12*(3), 45–57.

Behan, C. (2020). The benefits of meditation and mindfulness practices during times of crisis such as COVID-19. *Irish Journal of Psychological Medicine, 37*, 1–3.

Black, D. S. (2010). Incorporating mindfulness within established theories of health behavior. *Complementary Health Practice Review, 15*(2), 108–109. https://doi.org/10.1177/1533210110387815

Bunjak, A., Černe, M., & Schölly, E. L. (2022). Exploring the past, present, and future of the mindfulness field: A multitechnique bibliometric review. *Frontiers in Psychology, 13*, 792599.

Cherkin, D. C., Sherman, K. J., Balderson, B. H., Cook, A. J., Anderson, M. L., & Turner, J. A. (2016). Effectiveness of mindfulness-based stress reduction vs. cognitive behavioral therapy for chronic low back pain in adults. *JAMA Internal Medicine, 176*(3), 329–337.

Davidson, R. J., Kabat-Zinn, J., Schumacher, J., Rosenkranz, M., Muller, D., Santorelli, S. F., & Sheridan, J. F. (2003). Alterations in brain and immune function produced by mindfulness meditation. *Psychosomatic Medicine, 65*(4), 564–570.

Ghaffari, M. (2019). Prescribing mindfulness for heart health. *Online Journal of Complementary & Alternative Medicine*, 1–8. https://doi.org/10.33552/OJCAM.2019.02.000532

Goyal, M., Singh, S., Sibinga, E. M. S., et al. (2014). Meditation programs for psychological stress and well-being: A systematic review and meta-analysis. *JAMA Internal Medicine, 174*(3), 357–368.

Green, A. A., & Kinchen, E. (2021). The effects of mindfulness meditation on stress and burnout in nurses. *Journal of Holistic Nursing, 39*, 356–368.

Greeson, J. M. (2009). Mindfulness research update: 2008. *Complementary Health Practice Review, 14*(1), 10–18. https://doi.org/10.1177/1533210108329862

Hofmann, S. G., Sawyer, A. T., Witt, A. A., & Oh, D. (2010). The effect of mindfulness-based therapy on anxiety and depression: A meta-analytic review. *Journal of Consulting and Clinical Psychology, 78*(2), 169–183.

Hölzel, B. K., Carmody, J., Vangel, M., Congleton, C., Yerramsetti, S. M., Gard, T., & Lazar, S. W. (2011). Mindfulness practice leads to increases in regional brain gray matter density. *Psychiatry Research: Neuroimaging, 191*(1), 36–43.

Kabat-Zinn, J. (1994). *Wherever you go, there you are: Mindfulness meditation in everyday life*. Hyperion.

Kim, D. J. (2022). Mapping the mindfulness: A literature review of mindfulness in educational field. *Open Education Studies, 4*, 136–147.

Luders, E., Toga, A. W., Lepore, N., & Gaser, C. (2009). The underlying anatomical correlates of long-term meditation: Larger hippocampal and frontal volumes of gray matter. *NeuroImage, 45*(3), 672–678.

Ott, M. J. (2004). Mindfulness meditation: A path of transformation & healing. *Journal of Psychosocial Nursing and Mental Health Services, 42*(7), 22–29. https://doi.org/10.3928/02793695-20040701-04

Pascoe, M. C., Thompson, D. R., Jenkins, Z. M., & Ski, C. F. (2017). Mindfulness mediates the physiological markers of stress: Systematic review and meta-analysis. *Journal of Psychiatric Research, 95*, 156–178.

Querstret, D., Morison, L., Dickinson, S., Cropley, M., & John, M. (2020). Mindfulness-based stress reduction and mindfulness-based cognitive therapy for psychological health and well-being in nonclinical samples: A systematic review and meta-analysis. *International Journal of Stress Management, 27*, 394. https://doi.org/10.1037/str0000165

Ravalier, J. M., Wegrzynek, P., & Lawton, S. (2016). Systematic review: Complementary therapies and employee well-being. *Occupational Medicine, 66*(6), 428–436. https://doi.org/10.1093/occmed/kqw047

Schlechta Portella, C. F., Ghelman, R., Abdala, V., Schveitzer, M. C., & Afonso, R. F. (2021). Meditation: Evidence map of systematic reviews. *Frontiers in Public Health, 9*, 742715.

Soriano-Ayala, E., Amutio, A., Franco, C., & Mañas, I. (2020). Promoting a healthy lifestyle through mindfulness in university students: A randomized controlled trial. *Nutrients, 12*, 2450. https://doi.org/10.3390/nu12082450

Vasudeva, W., & Vasudeva, V. (2024). Yoga meditation: A path to holistic health and healing. *International Journal of Complementary & Alternative Medicine, 17*, 42. https://doi.org/10.15406/ijcam.2024.17.00682

Zeidan, F., Johnson, S. K., Diamond, B. J., David, Z., & Goolkasian, P. (2010). Mindfulness meditation improves cognition: Evidence of brief mental training. *Consciousness and Cognition, 19*(2), 597–605. https://doi.org/10.1016/j.concog.2010.03.014

Theories in Mindfulness Studies: A Narrative Review

Brajaballav Kar and Nilamadhab Kar

1 Introduction

Mindfulness has emerged as a critical concept in many fields including psychology, healthcare, leadership, and workplace well-being. Various constructs from different disciplines are examined for the link with mindfulness. Such linkages are examined from multiple theoretical lenses, ranging from cognitive and behavioral theories to self-determination and social cognitive theories.

Research involving mindfulness-based interventions and their effect on health, recovery, and well-being have increased. The Lay Theories of Health proposes that individuals have personal beliefs about health process and methods. The personal beliefs induce them to build frameworks by seeking suitable information from social media and engage in mindfulness content (Wang, Zhu, et al., 2023). The Interpersonal Theory of Suicide indicates that the feelings of perceived burdensomeness and failed belongingness contribute to suicidal thoughts and can be mitigated through a zest for life and mindful awareness (Collins et al., 2016). Mindfulness was also associated with vaccine hesitancy, during COVID-19

B. Kar (✉)
School of Management, KIIT University, Bhubaneswar, India
e-mail: braja.kar@ksom.ac.in

N. Kar
Department of Psychiatry, Black Country Healthcare NHS Foundation Trust, Wolverhampton, United Kingdom

Faculty of Contemplative and Behavioural Sciences, Sri Sri University, Cuttack, Odisha, India

Research Institute in Health Sciences, University of Wolverhampton, Wolverhampton, United Kingdom
e-mail: n.kar@nhs.net

S. Batra (ed.), *Health and Wellness for All: Navigating Pathways to a Better Life*, Advances in Mental Health and Addiction,
https://doi.org/10.1007/978-3-031-98979-7_2

pandemic (Mueller et al., 2022). The self-efficacy construct of the Social Cognitive Theory was related to the mindfulness-based eating behavior and increased adherence among diabetes patients (Harmiardillah et al., 2020, p. 2). Improved self-efficacy was also noted by imparting mindfulness-based education as proposed in the Self-efficacy Theory (Bayir & Aylaz, 2021). The Social Support Theory linked the reduction in postpartum depressive symptoms to perceived social support and mindfulness (Liu et al., 2022). Psychotherapy, well-being, and business can gain from an improved understanding of mindfulness and motivation (Ryan et al., 2021).

The Theory of mindful consumption links consumer behavior, information exchange, and education to understand the impact of materialism and demographics (Manchanda et al., 2023). Mindfulness helps in assessing objective threats and privacy concerns and influences online information sharing behavior, consistent with the Protection Motivation Theory (Ioannou et al., 2021).

Mindfulness research has expanded to organization studies as well, mostly through the link between mindfulness and well-being. Self-determination Theory (SDT) proposes that the motivation growth stems from the psychological needs such as autonomy, competence, and relatedness. These needs prompt actions toward intrinsic or extrinsic goals, influencing overall quality of life or well-being (Schultz et al., 2015). However, mindfulness is differentially related to different types of motivations, facilitates autonomous forms of motivation, and influences well-being and prosociality (Martin et al., 2017). A mindful approach and the fulfillment of basic psychological needs foster positive employee attitudes and self-determination (Zeshan et al., 2022). Monitor and Acceptance Theory suggests that mindfulness reduces organizational role stress, like personal inadequacy and self-role distance but has little impact on role erosion and overload, showing limited effectiveness for certain stressors (Warrier et al., 2022). Implicit mindfulness theory (IMT) refers to individuals' personal beliefs about what it means to be mindful (Kong & Jolly, 2019). Implicit mindfulness influences employees' behaviors, such as deviance, and in-role actions. Role conflict increases burnout and turnover intentions and job demands can drain energy, as per the demands-resources model. Higher mindfulness can reduce frustration, acting as a buffer against job-related stress (Olafsen et al., 2021). The High-Reliability Organizations (HROs) Theory suggests that extreme focus on failure, reluctance to simplify, operational sensitivity, resilience, and expertise can increase performance but this heightened mindfulness can be stressful (Ault & Brandley, 2023).

The Affective Events Theory suggests that cognitive behavior is a better predictor of work performance and satisfaction, compared to affective behavior. Mindfulness moderates the relationship between events and well-being, improving mental health and overall well-being in the workplace (Junça-Silva et al., 2021). An extension to the Broaden and Build Theory and the Conservation of Resources Theory suggests that respectful engagement enhances the positive relationship between team mindfulness and team commitment engagement (Rusdi & Wibowo, 2022).

The Theory of Planned Behavior (TPB) explains intentions to try mindfulness-based practices (Jones et al., 2022). Conscientiousness links attitude, subjective norms, and perceived behavior control with mindfulness (Kim et al., 2022). TPB and Temporal Self-Regulation Theory predict engagement in mindfulness (Crandall et al., 2019). Mindfulness moderates the relationship between intentions, attitudes, social influences, or perceived control, even for habit-based routine activities (Chatzisarantis & Hagger, 2007).

2 Research Objectives

Mindfulness research is multi-disciplinary and uses different theories to explain emotion, cognition, health, behavior, social influence, and well-being among others. This interdisciplinary perspective consolidates research and theories together to explicate complex processes. Thus, the broader objective of this study is to identify various theories used in mindfulness research in different disciplines. The specific objectives are to understand similarity or divergence among theories and to compare different measurement approaches and scales used in research. Identifying possible research directions is also one of the objectives. This narrative review explores the integration of mindfulness into diverse disciplines and provides an understanding of the theoretical frameworks that underpin its applications.

3 Methodology

A search conducted in the SCOPUS database on October 23, 2023, with "theory" AND "Mindfulness" as keywords, in the English language, without mentioning period resulted in 143 articles. Articles were evaluated for their theoretical bases in their research. Articles that discussed theoretical basis substantially in their methodology or findings were included in this narrative review. Representative articles with common theoretical bases were included. Seventy-six articles qualified for inclusion. The conceptual frameworks used in these articles are presented in the results.

4 Results

4.1 Physiological Basis of Mindfulness

The neural basis of mindfulness is explained by the Predictive and Reactive Control systems theory (PARC). The Default Mode Network is active at rest, while the anterior insula becomes active during task-related attention. These components, parts of homeostatic and behavioral control systems, alternate dominance to influence mental states, including mindfulness, mind-wandering, rumination, and self-experience (Tops et al., 2014). The Reinforcement Sensitivity Theory is related to PARC and proposes that the brain has a behavioral activation system (BAS), behavioral inhibition system (BIS), and fight/flight/freeze system (FFFS) that are responsible for individual differences in sensitivity to reward, punishment, and motivation. These systems are related to the trait mindfulness and together influence personality (Harnett et al., 2016). The goal-drive persistence of BAS was positively associated with mindfulness but BAS impulsivity negatively predicted acting with awareness aspect of mindfulness. Mindfulness was negatively associated with BIS, but did not show significant relationships with FFFS (Dolatyar & Walker, 2020).

Mindfulness theories often link to memory functions. Forgetting is not solely explained by memory decay, but also from interference from other long-term memories (Theory of Mental Interference). This theory supports the "threefold model of mindful wisdom." The model views cognitive process as unbiased by affect, distinct from mental interference, and shaped by personal and social experiences (Klebanova, 2022). Theory of Mind (ToM) or the Impaired Theory of Mind indicates that individuals have unique thoughts, feelings, beliefs, and mental states. Mindfulness and anxiety partially explain the variance in ToM (Balaban & Bilici, 2022). Mindfulness-based interventions effectively improves mental illnesses including psychosis (López-Navarro et al., 2022).

4.2 Developmental and Behavioral Theories

Childhood experience and language development processes are linked to mindfulness. Attachment Theory suggests that early childhood caregiver-child bond shapes mindfulness traits, in which secure, ambivalent, avoidant, and disorganized attachment styles play a role (Snyder et al., 2012). Relational Frame Theory links language development to emotions, as cognition creates arbitrary associations to stimulus, known as functional contextualism. Mindfulness disentangles these associations, evaluates verbal networks, and enhances perspective-taking (Edwards et al., 2017).

4.3 Cognitive Theories

Monitor and Acceptance Theory (MAT) provides a framework to explain and predict the diverse effects of mindfulness on attention, emotional reactivity, emotion regulation, and health outcomes. MAT suggests that attention monitoring enhances present-moment awareness but increases emotional reactivity while acceptance—defined as receptive non-interfering engagement with present—regulates emotions (Simione & Saldarini, 2023). Together, these skills improve mental and physical health outcomes (Lindsay & Creswell, 2019).

Attention monitoring increases affective reactivity, adding acceptance to it, and enhances well-being. Affective reactivity did not worsen well-being substantially, whereas acceptance significantly improved it. The lack of interaction between the attention monitoring and acceptance suggests that the positive effects of mindfulness depend primarily on acceptance (Simione et al., 2021). Acceptance reduces reactivity by regulating emotions, allowing individuals to experience present moment without interference, and balancing heightened emotional responses linked to enhanced cognitive awareness (Lindsay & Creswell, 2017). Removal of acceptance from mindfulness interventions greatly reduces their effectiveness (Lindsay & Creswell, 2019). Therapeutic benefits in the Acceptance and Commitment Therapy are explained by acceptance, diffusion, connecting with the present moment, and transcending the sense-of-self processes (Fletcher & Hayes, 2005).

Mindfulness to Meaning Theory (MMT) is a process model for mindful emotion regulation incorporating attentional control, decentering, broadened awareness, reappraisal, and positive affect constructs. Stressful events are reframed as benign, meaningful, or growth-promoting in the positive reappraisal process. The state mindfulness is significantly associated with frequent positive reappraisal, suggesting that they mutually reinforce each other in a positive feedback loop (Garland, Kiken, et al., 2017). Mindfulness training enhances awareness and the efficacy of reappraisal. Interpreting situations, fostering positive affect, and regulating emotions are improved due to a broadened awareness (Garland, Hanley, et al., 2017). The central proposition of Mindful Reappraisal Hypothesis is that a positive reappraisal improves well-being and emotional resilience (Hanley et al., 2021).

The MMT links trait mindfulness to higher life satisfaction. Life satisfaction encompasses core self-evaluation, positive and negative affect, and overall well-being. Trait mindfulness influences the core self-evaluation and negative affect, thereby affecting life satisfaction well-being (Li et al., 2022). Through meaning-making, mindfulness helps in posttraumatic recovery and growth (Williams et al., 2021).

Mindfulness contributes to enhanced eudaimonic well-being through various mediating processes, such as increased decentering, positive reappraisal, positive affect, and savoring. These effects can be observed even over short periods, making MMT processes relevant in daily life (Sgherza et al., 2022). The MMT proposes that emotion regulation promotes subjective well-being and relieves distress by decentering from initial stress appraisals, followed by positive reappraisal of life events, and linking a broadened state of awareness with narrative meaning-making (Wang, Garland, & Farb, 2023). Dispositional mindfulness reduces stress by decreasing negative affect and emotional reactivity more through decentering (non-judging) but its impact on positive affect is smaller (Johnson et al., 2021). Cancer patients with higher levels of dispositional mindfulness were more attentive to positive experiences, frequently engaged in positive reappraisal, and experienced a greater sense of meaning in life (Garland, Thielking, et al., 2017).

The MMT is a dynamic model of emotion regulation through cognitive-affective mechanisms that triggers upward spirals of decentering, attentional broadening, positive reappraisal, and savoring, leading to self-transcendence. Savoring facilitates absorptive experiences, self-transcendent emotions, and nondual awareness restructure reward processing, highlighting how mindfulness fosters well-being through cognitive and emotional transformation (Garland & Fredrickson, 2019).

4.4 Theories About Self and Others

Buddhist philosophy of mindfulness suggests that the belief of "no self" improves well-being, belief in having a "self" causes human suffering (Giles, 2019). Self-theories propose that mindfulness, as a dispositional quality of non-judgmental awareness, contrasts with emotional and cognitive biases. Individuals with less biased self-theories exhibit higher levels of dispositional mindfulness (Hanley et al., 2015).

Equanimity, as the separation of desire from both current and anticipated experiences in the Decoupling Model of Equanimity, is a similar proposition to mindfulness. Equanimity arises when there is a deliberate attitude of accepting experiences regardless of their nature. Mindfulness-based interventions promotes equanimity by intentional acceptance of all experiences (Hadash et al., 2016). Since individuals go through various mental states, the Whole Trait Theory (WTT) views mindfulness as both a momentary state fluctuating significantly across different contexts and an enduring trait. The enduring nature is reflected in the predominant distribution of states (Warren et al., 2023). The Broaden and Build theory proposes that positive emotions extend and strengthen psychological, social, cognitive, and physical resources, linking life satisfaction to mindfulness and the search for meaning (Dong & Geng, 2023).

4.5 Context and Mindfulness

One view suggests that life-altering experiences, especially major stressors, heighten self-awareness and reduce social conditioning, fostering free will. Another emphasizes purposive self-development—enhancing self-regulation and mindfulness—as a way to exercise free will. Both views connect these experiences to greater autonomy, linking personal growth with free will. Relational Developmental Systems Theories (RSDTs) explain this individual variability through interpersonal interactions and "free will" being central to this framework (Aldwin, 2015).

Satisfaction influences subjective well-being and is influenced by the aspiration-achievement gap. Multiple Discrepancies Theory (MDT) proposes various gaps between the current situation and ideal state, from past self, aspiration, others in society, expectations, deserved outcomes, needs, social norms, and alternate possibilities. Mindfulness, as an intervening variable, mediates the relationship between these discrepancies and overall well-being (Jacob & Brinkerhoff, 1999).

Mindfulness practices are closely linked to the metacognitive reflections outlined in Theory U, particularly during the "presencing" stage, a time to connect with the present while considering the future. These reflections enhance attention modes by fostering greater clarity, focus, and authenticity in articulating purpose statements. The Theory U complements the discrepancy theory and relates to mindfulness by aligning with one's goals and intentions (Calia et al., 2018).

4.6 Decision-Making Theories

The Signal Detection Theory perspective on mindfulness indicates that the improvement in attention and memory can be from a reduced response bias rather than actual memory sensitivity. The non-judging aspect of mindfulness reduces bias, but does not enhance memory sensitivity. Mindfulness affects memory through decision-making rather than directly improving information encoding (Rosenstreich & Ruderman, 2016). Avoiding thoughts or feelings often fail, making them more frequent and intense. This effect is potentially linked to the trait of mindfulness. The Ironic Process Theory explains it as a paradoxical cognitive model. Different mindfulness profiles and related mind control processes produce different levels of well-being. A judgmentally observing profile displays consistent low well-being compared to the non-judgmentally aware profile (Lee et al., 2024). Mind-wandering and mindfulness are explained through the Dual-System Theory. It is explained in cyber loafing where individuals intend to use smart phone for assistance at work, but are unable to use due to passive mind-wandering. This is due to the dual systems of mind where mindfulness can regulate individual behavior (Chen et al., 2023). Mind-wandering acts as noise, while being mindful improves memory sensitivity. It can also be linked to attention span or manage cognition overload. Attention improves the signal or reduces the noise but in a high noise situation, it can cause cognition overload resulting in chronic mindfulness. The Theory of Digital Mindfulness argues that self-monitoring can be objectively defined, systematically measured, and practically supported by digital tools and technologies, indicating that the mindful use of digital technologies can influence mindfulness (Abhari et al., 2021).

4.7 Potential Drawbacks

Mindfulness is not necessarily beneficial always or in every context. The High-Reliability Organization theory links high performance to a chronic mindfulness resulting in hypervigilance, mental fatigue, and overwhelming responsibility due to intense focus. To counter this, mindfulness practices should include coping strategies like stress reframing, seeking therapy, and engaging in cathartic expression to ensure better sense-making and trust in organizations (Ault & Brandley, 2023). Theories linked to mindfulness research identified in this study are presented in Table 1.

Table 1 List of theories linked to mindfulness research

Theories
1. Affective events theory
2. Attachment theory
3. Broaden and build theory
4. Conservation of resources theory
5. Decoupling model of equanimity
6. Dual-system theory
7. Generalizability theory
8. Grounded theory
9. High-reliability organizations theory
10. Implicit mindfulness theory
11. Ironic process theory
12. Item response theory
13. Lay theories of health
14. Mindfulness to meaning theory
15. Monitor and acceptance theory
16. Multiple discrepancies theory
17. Predictive and reactive control systems theory
18. Reinforcement sensitivity theory
19. Relational developmental systems theories
20. Relational frame theory
21. Self-determination theory
22. Self-efficacy theory
23. Self-theories
24. Signal detection theory
25. Social cognitive theory
26. Social support theory
27. Temporal self-regulation theory
28. Theory of digital mindfulness
29. Theory of mental interference
30. Theory of mind
31. Theory of mindful consumption
32. Theory of planned behavior (TPB)
33. Theory of suicide
34. Theory U
35. Whole trait theory

4.8 Methods and Scales in Extant Research

4.8.1 Methodology

Grounded Theory (GT) and its variants are most prominent approaches used in mindfulness research. It was used to explore mindfulness role in coping with interruptions (Reyes, 2022), facilitating personal transitions (Long et al., 2016), integrating with expressive arts (Rieger et al., 2023), supporting moral development in the workplace (Dhaka et al., 2022), understanding the effect of mindfulness on corporate risk mitigation (Simha & Kishore, 2011), and assisting individuals with substance use disorders (Himelstein et al., 2014). Constructivist GT was used to investigate mindfulness teaching practices (Braun et al., 2023; Hilert & Haskins, 2022) and GT with an interpretivist lens identified concentration and self-control as key leadership attributes (Babu et al., 2022).

Health-related mindfulness research using GT was used to understand how mindfulness promotes mental health (Mason, 2002), aids cognitive therapy (Irving et al., 2014; Langdon et al., 2011; Smith et al., 2015), and navigates countertransference in therapeutic relationships (Millon & Halewood, 2015). It was used to develop a theory of engagement explaining the role of mindfulness in group therapy (McHale et al., 2018). The Generalizability theory (G-theory) was used to assess the Interpersonal Mindfulness Scale (Chalmers et al., 2021), and the Toronto Mindfulness Scale (TMS) (Medvedev et al., 2017) highlighted the complexity of trait, state, and the influence of occasion on mindfulness.

The use of Grounded Theory in mindfulness research points to the attempt to identify constructs, interactions, and theory building. These efforts advance the understanding of mindfulness and its effects across various domains. It also points to consistent development and fluidity in current research methods.

4.8.2 Scales

Scales used in mindfulness studies indicate the diversity of measurement, nuances of constructs, contexts, and objectives of those studies (Table 2). Psychometric properties of mindfulness scales are evaluated using Item response theory and G-Theory. There are various mindfulness scales used in research, e.g. the Child and Adolescent Mindfulness Measure (Chiesi et al., 2017), the Five-Facet Mindfulness Questionnaire (FFMQ 39-, 24-, and 15-item scale), (Pelham III et al., 2019), etc. While the FFMQ-39 and FFMQ-18 have been found reliable in assessing trait mindfulness (Truong et al., 2020), the subscale "automatic inattentiveness" of the Mindful Attention Awareness Scale (MAAS) provides the most significant information about the latent mindfulness trait (Padhi et al., 2024; Van Dam et al., 2010).

Table 2 Different mindfulness scales used in research

Scale	Reference	Descriptions
Langer mindfulness scale (LMS)	(Langer, 1989)	21 items; Dimensions: novelty seeking, novelty producing, engagement, and flexibility. Measures dispositional mindfulness.
Self-regulation scale (SRS)	(Schwarzer et al., 1999)	Measures dispositional mindfulness, 10 items
Core self-evaluations scale	(Judge et al., 2003)	12 items, measures person's fundamental beliefs about themselves. Four main traits are included, e.g. self-esteem, generalized self-efficacy, locus of control, and emotional stability
Mindful attention awareness scale	(Brown & Ryan, 2003)	15 items, specifically focuses on the frequency of mindful states in day-to-day life.
Kentucky inventory of mindfulness skills	(Baer et al., 2004)	Skills: Observing, describing, acting with awareness, and accepting without judgment. 39 items
Five-facet mindfulness questionnaire (FFMQ)	(Baer et al., 2006)	Facets: Observing, describing, acting with awareness, non-judging of inner experience, non-reactivity to inner experience—39 items
Freiburg mindfulness inventory	(Walach et al., 2006)	14 items, measures mindfulness in daily life; present-moment focus and non-judgmental acceptance are dimensions.
Cognitive and affective mindfulness scale-R	(Feldman et al., 2007)	10 items; key components are present-moment attention, awareness, acceptance, and present-focus (not past or future).
Five-facet mindfulness Questionnaire	(Bohlmeijer et al., 2011)	Facets: Observing, describing, acting with awareness, non-judging of inner experience, non-reactivity to inner experience—15 items
Implicit mindfulness scale	(Kong & Jolly, 2019)	3 items, indirect measure, focusses on mindfulness-related tendencies as implicit awareness and implicit acceptance

5 Discussion

In this narrative review, we find that mindfulness is primarily understood through physiological, developmental, behavioral, cognitive, and social-interaction perspectives. Multi-disciplinary attempts are made to understand mindfulness from diverse theoretical perspectives to explicate cognition, self-regulation, human behavior, and well-being. The application of grounded theory and scale development efforts shows the mindfulness research is evolving (Sgherza et al., 2022; Simione & Saldarini, 2023).

Mindfulness research focuses on three theories such as the MAT, MMT, and the Implicit Mindfulness Theory. The link suggests that the acceptance and meaning-making creates the implicit mindfulness. Meaning-making, or decoupling emotions from habitual reactions requires a cognitive reappraisal. The decoupling model of equanimity also indicates a deliberate attitude to accept experience irrespective of their nature (Fig. 1).

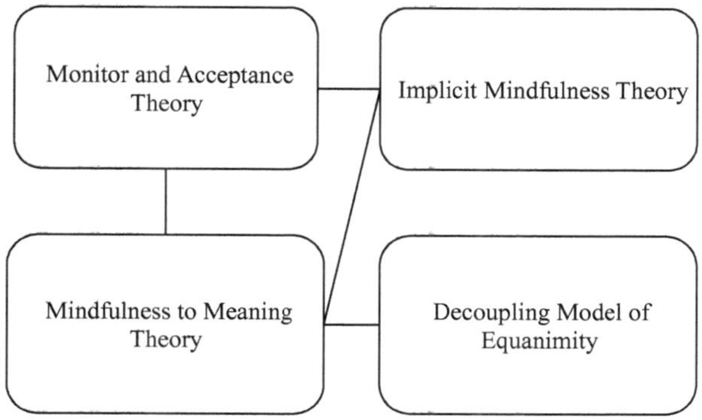

Fig. 1 Linkages in mindfulness theories

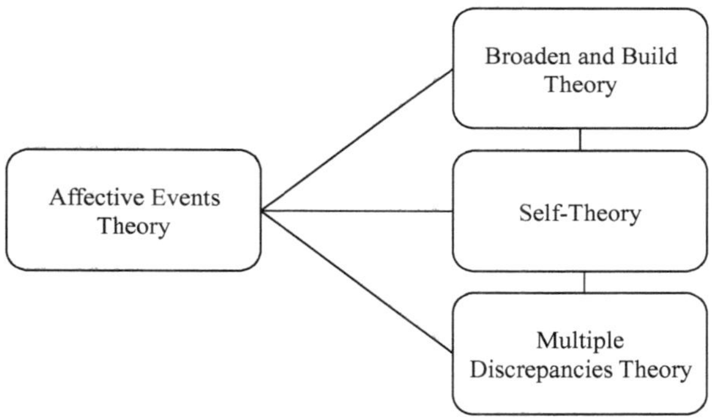

Fig. 2 Interaction of events and individuals in mindfulness

The influence of events on mindfulness is explained through Fig. 2. Both positive and negative emotions influence an individual to evaluate their own mindfulness model, to evaluate self, understand discrepancies, build upon the positive experiences, and strengthen psychological, cognitive, and physical resources, as suggested in the Broaden and Build theory, thereby influencing mindfulness.

Figure 3 depicts the relationship of theories from the memory, signal detection, and persistence of undesirable thought perspective. Some failure of memory could be from an interference from other long-term memory, and the efficacy of mindfulness is from the heightened sensitivity to appropriate signal (removing bias and making a choice), as proposed in Signal Detection Theory. These two perspectives link the persistence of thought that individuals avoid.

The association between theories involving cognitive processes, mental states, control systems, relational systems, learning and development, motivation, self-regulation, individual agency or interpersonal dynamics, and systemic changes are depicted in Fig. 4. The Theory of Mind proposes individuals to have unique thoughts, feelings, beliefs, and mental states. This links to the homeostatic and the task-related attention division proposed in the Predictive and Reactive Control Systems Theory. The Relational Development Systems Theory also indicates that life changing

Fig. 3 Signal or information theories linked to mindfulness

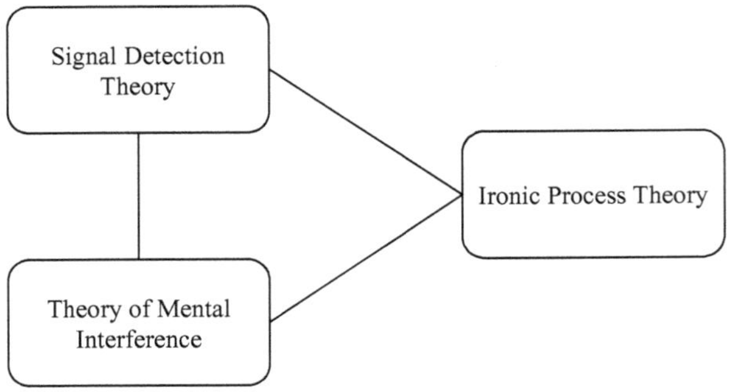

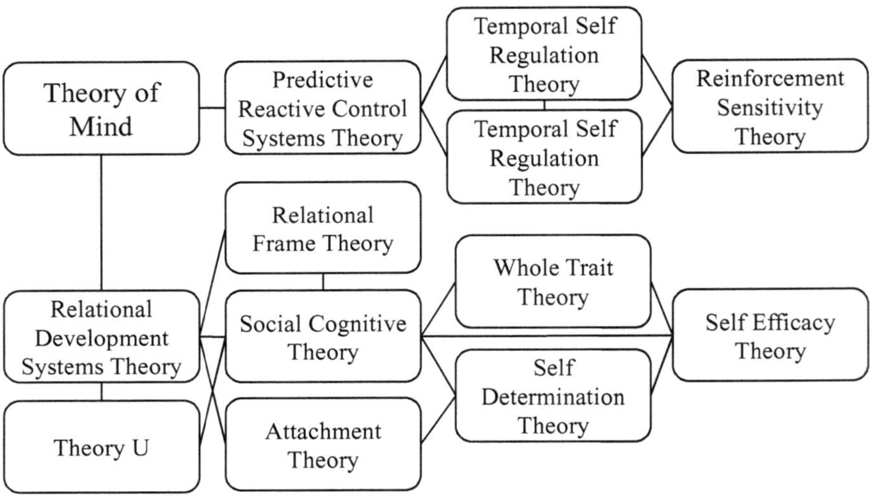

Fig. 4 Link of systemic and individual theories associated with mindfulness

experiences can reduce social conditioning and improve self-development, regulation, and mindfulness. The temporal self-regulation also indicates a control system perspective. The Dual System Theory extends the control system idea from a cognitive perspective. The sensitivity toward reward, punishment, and motivation is suggested from multi-system and regulation perspective as indicated in Fig. 4.

The Relational Developmental Systems theory and Relational Frame Theory connects with the social cognition perspective linking to mindfulness. Further, the social cognition aspect extends to the autonomy, competence, relatedness, and control aspects of the Self-Determination Theory. A predominant persistence of mindfulness states is indicated in the Whole Trait Theory which links to the Self-Efficacy Theory. The systemic and social perspective links the Theory U to others as indicated in fig. 4. These linkages present the broader schema of theories in mindfulness research.

The PARC theory links mindfulness behavior to neural substrates. The different types of behavioral activation systems and the individual sensitivity to reward and punishment also point to the physiological basis of mindfulness as proposed in the Reinforcement Sensitivity Theory. To an extent, the Attachment Theory explains mindfulness as the prior emotional bond between the caregiver and recipient. Similarly, the relational frame theory suggests the functional contextualism in language development and the attempt to disentangle any arbitrary link between language and emotion to cause mindfulness. The Relational Developmental Systems Theories (RSDTs) propose that an individual's relationship with context and the exercise of "free will" create awareness of choices and influence mindfulness. Theory U extends the argument by proposing that mindfulness is the metacognitive reflection due to enhanced attention modes. Thus, the nature versus nurture debate is evidenced in mindfulness research.

Grounded theory, Item response theory, and the Generalizability theory were mostly used for the development and validation of mindfulness aspects and were not included in the model. Similarly, the Theory of Planned Behavior (TPB), Social Support Theory, Theory of Mindful Consumption, Conservation of Resources Theory, Theory of Digital Mindfulness, Lay Theories of Health, and the Theory of Suicide were considered from the perspective of application of mindfulness and were not included in linking models.

5.1 *Implications*

Mindfulness-based interventions have shown good results in therapeutic settings, including mental and physical health, promoting well-being. Mindfulness practice can also lead to personal development, developing free will, self-awareness, and decision-making. Application of mindfulness practices also has shown results in education and workplace well-being. Therefore, understanding how mindfulness works through different theories is going to be crucial. At the same time, adverse effects of extreme level of mindfulness need to be understood.

5.2 *Limitations*

Articles for this research were identified from SCOPUS database only. However, this research identified around 35 theories or models that could be reasonable considering the search strings used.

6 Future Scope

The potential and mechanism of mindfulness improving health and well-being are the larger research questions being investigated. Future research can consider integrating constructs of different theories to converge our understanding. The possibility that mindfulness causes self-efficacy perception requires research. Convergence between the Signal Detection Theory, Dual-System Theory, and Ironic Process Theory is likely to bring clarity in the mechanisms of mindfulness.

The long-term effects of a consistent and stable pattern of mindfulness, along with its unique relationship to personality traits, life goals, well-being, and life satisfaction can significantly influence the acceptability of mindfulness-based practices. Investigating mindfulness in combination with other theories and constructs can enhance our understanding of well-being and life satisfaction.

7 Conclusion

The research interest in the Buddhist concept of mindfulness is emerging primarily for its influence on well-being. This review identifies state and trait mindfulness, memory, emotions, attention, decision-making, language and meaning-making, stress, self-efficacy, motivation, life satisfaction, information sharing, and consumption behavior as some of the research focus areas. Divergent theories, constructs, and measurement tools indicate attempt to consolidate and understand mindfulness comprehensively.

References

Abhari, K., Klase, M., Koobchehr, F., Olivares, F., Pesavento, M., Sosa, L., & Vaghefi, I. (2021). Toward a theory of digital mindfulness: A case of smartphone-based self-monitoring. *12783 LNCS*, 549–561. https://doi.org/10.1007/978-3-030-77750-0_35

Aldwin, C. M. (2015). How can developmental systems theories cope with free will? The importance of stress-related growth and mindfulness. *Research in Human Development, 12*(3–4), 189–195. https://doi.org/10.1080/15427609.2015.1068042

Ault, M., & Brandley, B. (2023). The human cost of chronic mindfulness in U.S. law enforcement: Toward a more nuanced understanding of HRO theory. *Journal of Applied Communication Research, 51*(1), 18–36. https://doi.org/10.1080/00909882.2022.2118547

Babu, V., Kumar, A., & Kumar, V. (2022). Exploring mindfulness and leadership development: Lessons learnt using grounded theory through the study of the performing arts. *FIIB Business Review*. https://doi.org/10.1177/23197145221088643

Baer, R. A., Smith, G. T., & Allen, K. B. (2004). Assessment of mindfulness by self-report: The Kentucky inventory of mindfulness skills. *Assessment, 11*(3), 191–206. https://doi.org/10.1177/1073191104268029

Baer, R. A., Smith, G. T., Hopkins, J., Krietemeyer, J., & Toney, L. (2006). Using self-report assessment methods to explore facets of mindfulness. *Assessment, 13*(1), 27–45. https://doi.org/10.1177/1073191105283504

Balaban, G., & Bilici, M. (2022). Anxiety and theory of mind: A moderated mediation model of mindfulness and gender. *PsyCh Journal, 11*(4), 510–519. https://doi.org/10.1002/pchj.536

Bayir, B., & Aylaz, R. (2021). The effect of mindfulness-based education given to individuals with substance-use disorder according to self-efficacy theory on self-efficacy perception. *Applied Nursing Research, 57*. https://doi.org/10.1016/j.apnr.2020.151354

Bohlmeijer, E., ten Klooster, P. M., Fledderus, M., Veehof, M., & Baer, R. (2011). Psychometric properties of the five facet mindfulness questionnaire in depressed adults and development of a short form. *Assessment, 18*(3), 308–320. https://doi.org/10.1177/1073191111408231

Braun, S. E., Mladen, S., Crawford, M., Edwards, S., & Kinser, P. (2023). A constructivist grounded theory exploration of Mindfulness for Healthcare Professional students. *Complementary Therapies in Clinical Practice, 50*. https://doi.org/10.1016/j.ctcp.2022.101689

Brown, K. W., & Ryan, R. M. (2003). The benefits of being present: Mindfulness and its role in psychological well-being. *Journal of Personality and Social Psychology, 84*(4), 822–848. https://doi.org/10.1037/0022-3514.84.4.822

Calia, R. C., De Oliveira, M. S. B., & Demarzo, M. M. P. (2018). Mindfulness and theory U for the professional sense of purpose. *Revista de Administracao Mackenzie, 19*(5), eRAMG180021. https://doi.org/10.1590/1678-6971/eRAMG180021

Chalmers, R. A., Pratscher, S. D., Bettencourt, B. A., & Medvedev, O. N. (2021). Applying generalizability theory to differentiate between trait and state in the interpersonal mindfulness scale (IMS). *Mindfulness, 12*(3), 613–622. https://doi.org/10.1007/s12671-020-01520-5

Chatzisarantis, N. L. D., & Hagger, M. S. (2007). Mindfulness and the intention-behavior relationship within the theory of planned behavior. *Personality and Social Psychology Bulletin, 33*(5), 663–676. https://doi.org/10.1177/0146167206297401

Chen, Q., Gong, Y., Lu, Y., & Chau, P. Y. K. (2023). How mindfulness decreases cyberloafing at work: A dual-system theory perspective. *European Journal of Information Systems, 32*(5), 841–857. https://doi.org/10.1080/0960085X.2022.2067490

Chiesi, F., Dellagiulia, A., Lionetti, F., Bianchi, G., & Primi, C. (2017). Using item response theory to explore the psychometric properties of the italian version of the child and adolescent mindfulness measure (CAMM). *Mindfulness, 8*(2), 351–360. https://doi.org/10.1007/s12671-016-0604-y

Collins, K. R. L., Best, I., Stritzke, W. G. K., & Page, A. C. (2016). Mindfulness and zest for life buffer the negative effects of experimentally-induced perceived burdensomeness and thwarted belongingness: Implications for theories of suicide. *Journal of Abnormal Psychology, 125*(5), 704–714. https://doi.org/10.1037/abn0000167

Crandall, A., Cheung, A., Young, A., & Hooper, A. P. (2019). Theory-based predictors of mindfulness meditation mobile app usage: A survey and cohort study. *JMIR mHealth and uHealth, 7*(3). https://doi.org/10.2196/10794

Dhaka, H., Gupta, R. K., & Sharma, T. (2022). Moral development at the workplace through buddhist mindfulness meditation: A grounded theory study. *Business Perspectives and Research, 12*, 224. https://doi.org/10.1177/22785337221132612

Dolatyar, K., & Walker, B. R. (2020). Reinforcement sensitivity theory and mindfulness. *Personality and Individual Differences, 163*. https://doi.org/10.1016/j.paid.2020.110089

Dong, X., & Geng, L. (2023). The role of mindfulness and meaning in life in adolescents' dispositional awe and life satisfaction: The broaden-and-build theory perspective. *Current Psychology, 42*(33), 28911–28924. https://doi.org/10.1007/s12144-022-03924-z

Edwards, D. J., McEnteggart, C., Barnes-Holmes, Y., Lowe, R., Evans, N., & Vilardaga, R. (2017). The impact of mindfulness and perspective-taking on implicit associations toward the elderly: A relational frame theory account. *Mindfulness, 8*(6), 1615–1622. https://doi.org/10.1007/s12671-017-0734-x

Feldman, G., Hayes, A., Kumar, S., Greeson, J., & Laurenceau, J.-P. (2007). Mindfulness and emotion regulation: The development and initial validation of the cognitive and affective mindfulness scale-revised (CAMS-R). *Journal of Psychopathology and Behavioral Assessment, 29*(3), 177–190. https://doi.org/10.1007/s10862-006-9035-8

Fletcher, L., & Hayes, S. C. (2005). Relational frame theory, acceptance and commitment therapy, and a functional analytic definition of mindfulness. *Journal of Rational - Emotive and Cognitive - Behavior Therapy, 23*(4), 315–336. https://doi.org/10.1007/s10942-005-0017-7

Garland, E. L., & Fredrickson, B. L. (2019). Positive psychological states in the arc from mindfulness to self-transcendence: Extensions of the Mindfulness-to-Meaning Theory and applications to addiction and chronic pain treatment. *Current Opinion in Psychology, 28*, 184–191. https://doi.org/10.1016/j.copsyc.2019.01.004

Garland, E. L., Hanley, A. W., Goldin, P. R., & Gross, J. J. (2017). Testing the mindfulness-to-meaning theory: Evidence for mindful positive emotion regulation from a reanalysis of longitudinal data. *PLoS One, 12*(12), e0187727. https://doi.org/10.1371/journal.pone.0187727

Garland, E. L., Kiken, L. G., Faurot, K., Palsson, O., & Gaylord, S. A. (2017). Upward spirals of mindfulness and reappraisal: Testing the mindfulness-to-meaning theory with autoregressive latent trajectory modeling. *Cognitive Therapy and Research, 41*(3), 381–392. https://doi.org/10.1007/s10608-016-9768-y

Garland, E. L., Thielking, P., Thomas, E. A., Coombs, M., White, S., Lombardi, J., & Beck, A. (2017). Linking dispositional mindfulness and positive psychological processes in cancer survivorship: A multivariate path analytic test of the mindfulness-to-meaning theory. *Psycho-Oncology, 26*(5), 686–692. https://doi.org/10.1002/pon.4065

Giles, J. (2019). Relevance of the no-self theory in contemporary mindfulness. *Current Opinion in Psychology, 28*, 298–301. https://doi.org/10.1016/j.copsyc.2019.03.016

Hadash, Y., Segev, N., Tanay, G., Goldstein, P., & Bernstein, A. (2016). The decoupling model of equanimity: Theory, measurement, and test in a mindfulness intervention. *Mindfulness, 7*(5), 1214–1226. https://doi.org/10.1007/s12671-016-0564-2

Hanley, A. W., de Vibe, M., Solhaug, I., Farb, N., Goldin, P. R., Gross, J. J., & Garland, E. L. (2021). Modeling the mindfulness-to-meaning theory's mindful reappraisal hypothesis: Replication with longitudinal data from a randomized controlled study. *Stress and Health, 37*(4), 778–789. https://doi.org/10.1002/smi.3035

Hanley, A., Garland, E., Canto, A., Warner, A., Hanley, R., Dehili, V., & Proctor, A. (2015). Dispositional mindfulness and bias in self-theories. *Mindfulness, 6*(2), 202–207. https://doi.org/10.1007/s12671-013-0245-3

Harmiardillah, S., Krisnana, I., & Priastana, I. K. A. (2020). The effect of mindfulness-based eating exercise with social cognitive theory (Sct) approach to self-efficacy and dietary adherence of diabetes mellitus type 2. *International Journal of Pharmaceutical Research, 13*(1), 413–419. https://doi.org/10.31838/ijpr/2021.13.01.078

Harnett, P. H., Reid, N., Loxton, N. J., & Lee, N. (2016). The relationship between trait mindfulness, personality and psychological distress: A revised reinforcement sensitivity theory perspective. *Personality and Individual Differences, 99*, 100–105. https://doi.org/10.1016/j.paid.2016.04.085

Hilert, A. J., & Haskins, N. (2022). Teaching mindfulness in prison settings: A grounded theory of strategies to promote engagement and empowerment. *Journal of Offender Rehabilitation, 61*(1), 1–19. https://doi.org/10.1080/10509674.2021.2017384

Himelstein, S., Saul, S., Garcia-Romeu, A., & Pinedo, D. (2014). Mindfulness training as an intervention for substance user incarcerated adolescents: A pilot grounded theory study. *Substance Use and Misuse, 49*(5), 560– 570. https://doi.org/10.3109/10826084.2013.852580

Ioannou, A., Tussyadiah, I., & Marshan, A. (2021). Dispositional mindfulness as an antecedent of privacy concerns: A protection motivation theory perspective. *Psychology and Marketing, 38*(10), 1766–1778. https://doi.org/10.1002/mar.21529

Irving, J. A., Park-Saltzman, J., Fitzpatrick, M., Dobkin, P. L., Chen, A., & Hutchinson, T. (2014). Experiences of health care professionals enrolled in mindfulness-based medical practice: A grounded theory model. *Mindfulness, 5*(1), 60–71. https://doi.org/10.1007/s12671-012-0147-9

Jacob, J. C., & Brinkerhoff, M. B. (1999). Mindfulness and subjective well-being in the sustainability movement: A further elaboration of multiple discrepancies theory. *Social Indicators Research, 46*(3), 341–368. https://doi.org/10.1023/A:1006941403481

Johnson, L. K., Nadler, R., Carswell, J., & Minda, J. P. (2021). Using the broaden-and-build theory to test a model of mindfulness, affect, and stress. *Mindfulness, 12*(7), 1696–1707. https://doi.org/10.1007/s12671-021-01633-5

Jones, S. M. W., Sherman, K. J., Bermet, Z., Palazzo, L. G., & Lewis, C. C. (2022). Theory of planned behavior and mindfulness intentions in chronic low back pain. *Mindfulness, 13*(12), 3145–3152. https://doi.org/10.1007/s12671-022-02022-2

Judge, T. A., Erez, A., Bono, J. E., & Thoresen, C. J. (2003). The core self-evaluations scale: Development of a measure. *Personnel Psychology, 56*(2), 303–331. https://doi.org/10.1111/j.1744-6570.2003.tb00152.x

Junça-Silva, A., Pombeira, C., & Caetano, A. (2021). Testing the affective events theory: The mediating role of affect and the moderating role of mindfulness. *Applied Cognitive Psychology, 35*(4), 1075–1081. https://doi.org/10.1002/acp.3843

Kim, S., Park, J. Y., & Chung, K. (2022). The relationship between the big five personality traits and the theory of planned behavior in using mindfulness mobile apps: Cross-sectional survey. *Journal of Medical Internet Research, 24*(11). https://doi.org/10.2196/39501

Klebanova, K. (2022). Rethinking mindfulness in education within two frameworks: Articulating the "threefold model of mindful wisdom" with the "theory of mental interference". *Religions, 13*(1). https://doi.org/10.3390/rel13010066

Kong, D. T., & Jolly, P. M. (2019). Lay beliefs about attention to and awareness of the present: Implicit mindfulness theory (IMT) and its workplace implications. *Journal of Business and Psychology, 34*(5), 685–707. https://doi.org/10.1007/s10869-018-9606-1

Langdon, S., Jones, F. W., Hutton, J., & Holttum, S. (2011). A grounded-theory study of mindfulness practice following mindfulness-based cognitive therapy. *Mindfulness, 2*(4), 270–281. https://doi.org/10.1007/s12671-011-0070-5

Langer, E. J. (1989). *Mindfulness*. De Capon Press.

Lee, J. H., Moon, Y. K., Lee, K.-S., & Beehr, T. A. (2024). The negative effect of solving the 'white bear' problem with mindfulness: Expansion and reconfirmation of mindfulness profiles based on ironic process theory. *Personality and Individual Differences, 217*. https://doi.org/10.1016/j.paid.2023.112447

Li, X., Ma, L., & Li, Q. (2022). How mindfulness affects life satisfaction: Based on the mindfulness-to-meaning theory. *Frontiers in Psychology, 13*. https://doi.org/10.3389/fpsyg.2022.887940

Lindsay, E. K., & Creswell, J. D. (2017). Mechanisms of mindfulness training: Monitor and acceptance theory (MAT). *Clinical Psychology Review, 51*, 48–59. https://doi.org/10.1016/j.cpr.2016.10.011

Lindsay, E. K., & Creswell, J. D. (2019). Mindfulness, acceptance, and emotion regulation: Perspectives from monitor and acceptance theory (MAT). *Current Opinion in Psychology, 28*, 120–125. https://doi.org/10.1016/j.copsyc.2018.12.004

Liu, C., Chen, H., Zhou, F., Long, Q., Wu, K., Lo, L.-M., Hung, T.-H., Liu, C.-Y., & Chiou, W.-K. (2022). Positive intervention effect of mobile health application based on mindfulness and social support theory on postpartum depression symptoms of puerperae. *BMC Women's Health, 22*(1). https://doi.org/10.1186/s12905-022-01996-4

Long, J., Briggs, M., Long, A., & Astin, F. (2016). Starting where I am: A grounded theory exploration of mindfulness as a facilitator of transition in living with a long-term condition. *Journal of Advanced Nursing, 72*(10). 2445–2456. https://doi.org/10.1111/jan.12998

López-Navarro, E., Fonseca-Pedrero, E., Errasti, J., & Al-Halabí, S. (2022). Mindfulness improves theory of mind in people experiencing psychosis: A pilot randomized clinical trial. *Psychiatry Research, 310*. https://doi.org/10.1016/j.psychres.2022.114440

Manchanda, P., Arora, N., Nazir, O., & Islam, J. U. (2023). Cultivating sustainability consciousness through mindfulness: An application of theory of mindful-consumption. *Journal of Retailing and Consumer Services, 75*. https://doi.org/10.1016/j.jretconser.2023.103527

Martin, J. J., Byrd, B., Wooster, S., & Kulik, N. (2017). Self-determination theory: The role of the health care professional in promoting mindfulness and perceived competence. *Journal of Applied Biobehavioral Research, 22*(4). https://doi.org/10.1111/jabr.12072

Mason, O. J. (2002). The application of mindfulness meditation in mental health: Can protocol analysis help triangulate a grounded theory approach? *Forum Qualitative Sozialforschung, 3*(1).

McHale, C., Hayward, M., & Jones, F. W. (2018). Building a grounded theory of engagement in mindfulness-based group therapy for distressing voices. *Qualitative Health Research, 28*(14), 2169–2182. https://doi.org/10.1177/1049732318789897

Medvedev, O. N., Krägeloh, C. U., Narayanan, A., & Siegert, R. J. (2017). Measuring Mindfulness: Applying Generalizability Theory to Distinguish between State and Trait. *Mindfulness, 8*(4), 1036–1046. https://doi.org/10.1007/s12671-017-0679-0

Millon, G., & Halewood, A. (2015). Mindfulness meditation and countertransference in the therapeutic relationship: A small-scale exploration of therapists' experiences using grounded theory methods. *Counselling and Psychotherapy Research, 15*(3), 188–196. https://doi.org/10.1002/capr.12020

Mueller, E. A., Suvanbenjakule, P., Lim, C. X., O'Brien, W. H., Chavanovanich, J., Jarukasemthawee, S., Pisitsungkagarn, K., & Suavansri, P. (2022). Coping with COVID-19: Survey data assessing psychological distress to COVID-19 and vaccine hesitancy with measures of theory of planned behavior, mindfulness, compassion, cultural orientation, and pandemic fatigue. *Data in Brief, 43*, 108390. https://doi.org/10.1016/j.dib.2022.108390

Olafsen, A. H., Niemiec, C. P., Deci, E. L., Halvari, H., Nilsen, E. R., & Williams, G. C. (2021). Mindfulness buffers the adverse impact of need frustration on employee outcomes: A self-determination theory perspective. *Journal of Theoretical Social Psychology, 5*(3), 283–296. https://doi.org/10.1002/jts5.93

Padhi, B., Kar, N., & Kar, B. (2024). Mindfulness in different sociodemographic strata: Partial validation of the mindful attention awareness scale in an indian sample. *Annals of Indian Psychiatry, 8*(4), 317. https://doi.org/10.4103/aip.aip_42_24

Pelham, W. E., III, Gonzalez, O., Metcalf, S. A., Whicker, C. L., Scherer, E. A., Witkiewitz, K., Marsch, L. A., & Mackinnon, D. P. (2019). Item response theory analysis of the five facet mindfulness questionnaire and its short forms. *Mindfulness, 10*(8), 1615–1628. https://doi.org/10.1007/s12671-019-01105-x

Reyes, A. T. (2022). The Process of Learning Mindfulness and Acceptance through the Use of a Mobile App Based on Acceptance and Commitment Therapy: A Grounded Theory Analysis. *Issues in Mental Health Nursing, 43*(1), 3–12. https://doi.org/10.1080/01612840.2021.1953652

Rieger, K. L., Hack, T. F., Duff, M. A., Campbell-Enns, H. J., & West, C. H. (2023). Integrating mindfulness and the expressive arts for meaning making in cancer care: A grounded theory of the processes, facilitators, and challenges. *Supportive Care in Cancer, 31*(8). https://doi.org/10.1007/s00520-023-07909-x

Rosenstreich, E., & Ruderman, L. (2016). Not sensitive, yet less biased: A signal detection theory perspective on mindfulness, attention, and recognition memory. *Consciousness and Cognition, 43*, 48–56. https://doi.org/10.1016/j.concog.2016.05.007

Rusdi, Z. M., & Wibowo, A. (2022). Team mindfulness, team commitment and team respectful engagement: The lens of the conservation of resources theory and the broaden-and-build theory. *Organization Management Journal, 19*(5), 189–199. https://doi.org/10.1108/OMJ-09-2021-1336

Ryan, R. M., Donald, J. N., & Bradshaw, E. L. (2021). Mindfulness and motivation: A process view using self-determination theory. *Current Directions in Psychological Science, 30*(4), 300–306. https://doi.org/10.1177/09637214211009511

Schultz, P. P., Ryan, R. M., Niemiec, C. P., Legate, N., & Williams, G. C. (2015). Mindfulness, work climate, and psychological need satisfaction in employee well-being. *Mindfulness, 6*(5), 971–985. https://doi.org/10.1007/s12671-014-0338-7

Schwarzer, R., Diehl, M., & Schmitz, G. S. (1999). Self-regulation scale [Dataset]. https://doi.org/10.1037/t01606-000.

Sgherza, T. R., DeMarree, K. G., & Naragon-Gainey, K. (2022). Testing the mindfulness-to-meaning theory in daily life. *Mindfulness, 13*(9), 2324–2336. https://doi.org/10.1007/s12671-022-01961-0

Simha, A., & Kishore, R. (2011). Social capital and IT as predicates of collective mindfulness and business risk mitigation: A grounded theory development. *ICIS, 2*, 1445–1462.

Simione, L., Raffone, A., & Mirolli, M. (2021). Acceptance, and not its interaction with attention monitoring, increases psychological well-being: Testing the monitor and acceptance theory of mindfulness. *Mindfulness, 12*(6), 1398–1411. https://doi.org/10.1007/s12671-021-01607-7

Simione, L., & Saldarini, F. (2023). A critical review of the monitor and acceptance theory of mindfulness. *Mindfulness, 14*(6), 1317–1328. https://doi.org/10.1007/s12671-023-02129-0

Smith, E. L., Jones, F. W., Holttum, S., & Griffiths, K. (2015). The process of engaging in mindfulness-based cognitive therapy as a partnership: A grounded theory study. *Mindfulness, 6*(3), 455–466. https://doi.org/10.1007/s12671-014-0278-2

Snyder, R., Shapiro, S., & Treleaven, D. (2012). Attachment theory and mindfulness. *Journal of Child and Family Studies, 21*(5), 709–717. https://doi.org/10.1007/s10826-011-9522-8

Tops, M., Boksem, M. A., Quirin, M., Ijzerman, H., & Koole, S. L. (2014). Internally directed cognition and mindfulness: An integrative perspective derived from predictive and reactive control systems theory. *Frontiers in Psychology, 5*(May). https://doi.org/10.3389/fpsyg.2014.00429

Truong, Q. C., Krägeloh, C. U., Siegert, R. J., Landon, J., & Medvedev, O. N. (2020). Applying generalizability theory to differentiate between trait and state in the five facet mindfulness questionnaire (FFMQ). *Mindfulness, 11*(4), 953–963. https://doi.org/10.1007/s12671-020-01324-7

Van Dam, N. T., Earleywine, M., & Borders, A. (2010). Measuring mindfulness? An item response theory analysis of the mindful attention awareness scale. *Personality and Individual Differences, 49*(7), 805–810. https://doi.org/10.1016/j.paid.2010.07.020

Walach, H., Buchheld, N., Buttenmüller, V., Kleinknecht, N., & Schmidt, S. (2006). Measuring mindfulness—The freiburg mindfulness inventory (FMI). *Personality and Individual Differences, 40*(8), 1543–1555. https://doi.org/10.1016/j.paid.2005.11.025

Wang, Y., Garland, E. L., & Farb, N. A. S. (2023). An experimental test of the mindfulness-to-meaning theory: Casual pathways between decentering, reappraisal, and well-being. *Emotion, 23*, 2243. https://doi.org/10.1037/emo0001252

Wang, X., Zhu, B., Guo, Q., Wang, W., & Zhao, R. (2023). Designing mindfulness information for interaction in social media: The role of information framing, health risk perception and lay theories of health. *Frontiers in Psychology, 13*. https://doi.org/10.3389/fpsyg.2023.1041016

Warren, M. T., Galla, B. M., & Grund, A. (2023). Using whole trait theory to unite trait and state mindfulness. *Journal of Research in Personality, 104*. https://doi.org/10.1016/j.jrp.2023.104372

Warrier, U., Foropon, C., & Chehimi, M. (2022). Examining the influence of mindfulness on organizational role stress (ORS): A monitor acceptance theory perspective. *International Journal of Manpower, 43*(2), 448–462. https://doi.org/10.1108/IJM-02-2021-0067

Williams, H., Skalisky, J., Erickson, T. M., & Thoburn, J. (2021). Posttraumatic growth in the context of grief: Testing the mindfulness-to-meaning theory. *Journal of Loss and Trauma, 26*(7), 611–623. https://doi.org/10.1080/15325024.2020.1855048

Zeshan, M., de La Villarmois, O., Rasool, S., & Niazi, A. R. K. (2022). The perfect moment is this one. The effect of mindfulness on employees: A perspective from self-determination theory. *International Journal of Organizational Analysis, 31*, 3617. https://doi.org/10.1108/IJOA-07-2022-3346

The Impact of AI-Driven Health & Wellness Programs on Employee Well-being and Organizational Performance: A Mixed-Methods Investigation

Elamurugan Balasundaram, Nagaraj Navalgund, P. Aranganathan, Sanjay V. Hanji, and Meghana Shashidhar

1 Introduction

The fast-paced advancement in artificial intelligence (AI) technologies has resulted in transformational change across different organizational functions including workplace wellness programs which appear to be the most promising areas (Chen et al., 2023; Desai et al., 2023). Organizations are increasingly realizing that employee well-being is linked to success; hence, there is a growing interest in traditional wellness initiatives being enhanced by AI capabilities (Tiwari & Waoo, 2024).

Recent studies have revealed the great economic burden of workplace stress and poor employee health globally, with estimations suggesting that stress-related absences alone cause a loss of more than $300 billion annually to organizations worldwide (Davidson, 2023). Traditional wellness programs suffer from low participation rates, limited customization options as well as inadequate data analytics

E. Balasundaram (✉)
Saveetha Institute of Medical and Technical Sciences, Chennai, India

N. Navalgund
KLE Technological University, Hubli, Karnataka, India
e-mail: nagaraj.n@kletech.ac.in

P. Aranganathan
Hallmark Business School, Tiruchirappalli, Tamilnadu, India
e-mail: aranganathan.p@gsb.co.in

S. V. Hanji
MIT Vishwaprayag University, Solapur, Maharashtra, India

M. Shashidhar
Brillio, Bengaluru, India

S. Batra (ed.), *Health and Wellness for All: Navigating Pathways to a Better Life*, Advances in Mental Health and Addiction,
https://doi.org/10.1007/978-3-031-98979-7_3

capacities among other issues like these (Williams et al., 2022). The use of AI technology can help solve this problem through tailored interventions, real-time monitoring and predictive analytics as seen among others (Bolpagni et al., 2024).

Integrating AI into workplace wellness marks a shift from reactive to proactive healthcare management (Anderson, 2022). Through the application of algorithms and big data analytics for machine learning, organizations can now personalize well-being recommendations, anticipate likely health threats in advance, and encourage early intervention strategies (Galetsi et al., 2019). Despite the increasing popularity of these AI-powered wellness solutions, there is still a lack of empirical research on their effectiveness (Harrison & Luna-Reyes, 2022).

Some scholars have carried out studies on some specific areas of the workplace wellness programs. For example, Howarth et al. (2018) illustrated the positive effects of digital health interventions on employee engagement while Thompson et al. (2023) investigated AI as mental health support systems. However, few broad-based studies of how AI-centered wellness initiatives contribute to both good worker welfare and organizational functioning are available (Wilson & Ross, 2024).

This gap is addressed by this study using mixed-methods approach across 150 medium-large sized firms. By building upon organizational health capital framework (Nuñez & Villanueva, 2011), we examine how implementation of AI-enabled initiatives in relation to corporate well-being has an impact on employee well-being and organizational performance indicators. The article specifically looks at how AI-driven wellness programs affect different outcomes like stress management, work–life balance productivity, or absenteeism rates.

Objectives of the research

- To evaluate how useful AI-driven wellness programs are in improving employee health and organization performance
- To identify what factors help and hinder effective implementation of AI-based healthy living systems
- To come up with workable plans for companies wishing to make use of AI in their fitness programs.

The study provides practical evidence on the transformative potential of artificial intelligence (AI) in workplace health. For researchers, it adds new knowledge to existing literature on corporate health management by including information about AI tools (Ferguson et al., 2023). For practitioners, it gives them an opportunity to improve planning and implementation of efficient AI-based wellness models which match organizational objectives while taking care of employees.

The rest of this paper is organized as follows: A broad survey on relevant scholarships will be presented first, followed by a description of our research approach. Next, we present our findings and discuss their implications for theory and practice. Lastly, we have concluded by providing suggestions for future research into possible applications in organizations.

2 Literature Review

2.1 *Evolution of Workplace Wellness Programs*

There have been major transformations since the 1970s in how people view workplace wellness (Thompson et al., 2023). Initially, they were more concerned with the health and safety of fellow workers, but currently psychological well-being, work–life balance, and other aspects are included (Yusuf et al., 2022). Mrazek et al. (2019) have, however, found that traditional wellness programs oftentimes have a difficult time keeping participants engaged over the long term or tailoring them to individuals. On this account, organizations feel compelled to adopt advanced technology-based ways of doing things (Chen et al., 2023).

2.2 *Artificial Intelligence in Healthcare and Wellness*

In the healthcare sector, as like in other industries, AI has shown great potential usefulness toward better health outcomes and service delivery (Hanji, Hungund, et al., 2023; Hanji, Navalgund, et al., 2023; Kulal et al., 2024). Specifically, Davidson et al. (2022) presented studies where machine learning algorithms made significant strides in early disease identification and risk scoring for preventable medical conditions. For example, Morande (2022) lists personalized health recommendations as one application of AI in the workplace wellness while predictive analytics for stress management is another one.

2.3 *Impact of AI-Driven Wellness Programs on Employee Health*

Presently, studies have shown that AI-powered wellness initiatives are effective for improving physical health parameters. In one research conducted by Bolpagni et al. (2024), organizations that implemented artificial intelligence-based programs experienced a 45% higher staff participation than those running traditional systems. Furthermore, longitudinal research done by Ferguson et al. (2023) indicated considerable improvements among the key health indicators including blood pressure and body mass index of participants in the program.

In recent times, there has been growing attention to the contribution of AI in managing mental illnesses. Harrison and Luna-Reyes (2022) explained how artificial intelligence-powered platforms can be used to detect signs of employee burnout and stress at an early stage. In terms of numbers, Bolpagni et al. (2024) discovered a decrease in stress-related leaves by approximately 40% in organizations utilizing AI-driven mental health support systems. This report is consistent with earlier works such as Zantvoort et al. (2023), which demonstrated that personalized mental health interventions have better outcomes compared to generic approaches.

2.4 Organizational Performance Metrics

Studies conducted on AI-driven wellness programs and organizational performance suggest promising outcomes. Another study carried out by Tiwari and Waoo (2024) showed a positive relationship between participating in wellness programs and productivity indices. Similarly, Pooja and Sareen (2024) posited that companies that engaged in AI-enhanced wellness were able to up their staff engagement levels by 30%.

Research has shown that AI-driven wellness programs have had a profound effect on attendance and retention. The Henderson et al. (2023) study shows that companies adopting these programs saw a reduction of 25% in unscheduled absenteeism. Furthermore, Galetsi et al. (2019) discovered that high-quality wellness programs resulted in fewer employees quitting the company as well as improved recruitment results.

2.5 Implementation Challenges and Success Factors

Effective implementation of AI-driven wellness programs requires robust technical infrastructure and data management capabilities (Davidson et al., 2023). Organizations must deal with issues pertaining to privacy, integration of systems, and introduction of technology (Ferguson et al., 2023). Wilson and Ross (2024) provide important insights regarding the primary technological requirements for successful execution encompassing robust architecture for storing sensitive data and ensuring smooth user interfaces without any interruptions.

The key success factors identified from several studies include cultural acceptance and leadership support. Anderson (2022) insists on the importance of creating a work environment supportive of employee's health. Slater et al. (2023) reveal how leadership approval along with appropriate communication approaches impacts significantly on program outcomes.

2.6 Gaps in Current Literature

Even though more and more evidence are coming forth on the effectiveness of wellness programs based on AI, some research gaps still show. Firstly, many studies explore big companies leaving out implications for smaller organizations. Secondly, long-term effects as well as return on investments' metrics are largely unexplored.

In conclusion, there has been little research in this area exploring the intersection between AI health initiatives and socio-demographic changes across different cultural contexts.

2.7 Theoretical Framework

This paper contributes to the Organizational Human Capital Theory that was put forward by Grossman (2000), which claims that investment in employee well-being directly affects the performance of an organization. Incorporating elements of the Technology Acceptance Model (Davis, 1987) and the Digital Health Intervention Framework (Emerson et al., 2023), we extend this framework by assessing how AI technologies mediate the relationship between wellness initiatives and organizational outcomes.

3 Methodology

3.1 Research Design

This study utilized a mixed-methods research design conducted over 24 months (April 2022 to March 2024), with both quantitative and qualitative approaches employed to gain a holistic understanding of impacts of AI-driven wellness programs (Thompson et al., 2023). The research design was a sequential explanatory strategy whereby quantitative data collection and analysis were followed by qualitative inquiry for deeper insights into findings (Pooja & Sareen, 2024).

3.2 Sample Selection and Characteristics

The research involved 60 medium-to-large organizations that were selected randomly in order to ensure various industrial and geographical representation. Medium (100–499 employees: 38 organizations) and large-sized (500+ employees: 22 organizations) enterprises characterized the sample. The distribution of industries included technology, healthcare, manufacturing, services, and retail at approximately 28%, 22%, 20%, 17%, and 13%, respectively. On investigation, these organizations were asked to have AI-driven well-being programs for at least 12 months before the study (Bolpagni et al., 2024).

3.3 Participant Sample

There was a total of 415 participants, who were in the employee group; there was also a control group with about 262 participants. HR managers' number was 31, whereas wellness program administrators were 17. Participants within each organization were chosen using systematic random sampling to control for factors such as age, job title, and organizational tenure (Henderson et al., 2023).

3.4 Data Collection Methods

3.4.1 Quantitative Data Collection

Employee surveys were one of the quantitative data collection methods. Other examples include performance metrics and health indicators. For instance, employee surveys involved quarterly standardized wellness assessment surveys, bi-annual employee engagement surveys, work–life balance assessment tools, stress and burnout measurement scales with Cronbach's $\alpha > 0.85$ on all instruments used (Cronbach's $\alpha > 0.85$). Performance metrics consisted of absenteeism rates, productivity indicators, healthcare utilization data, program participation rates, and wellness program usage analytics. Health indicators were aggregated health assessment data; measures for stress levels; physical activity indices; and sleep quality data. All health information collected was in compliance with HIPAA regulations as well as other relevant data protection laws.

3.4.2 Qualitative Data Collection

The qualitative methods of collecting information included focus groups, in-depth interviews, and observational data. There were 30 focus groups each consisting of 8–10 participants using a semi-structured discussion format that lasted 90 min per session and had been recorded then transcribed verbatim. In-depth interviews included 20 one-on-one interviews with HR managers as well as 15 interviews done with program administrators which lasted for 1 h each and followed a standardized interview protocol. Observational data captured the processes involved in implementing programs like how AI wellness platforms functioned from users' points of view and signs of organizational culture are present in it.

3.5 Data Analysis Procedures

Demographic and baseline data were subjected to descriptive statistics during quantitative data analysis, relationship testing entailed multiple regression analysis, causal pathway analysis involved structural equation modeling (SEM), mixed-effects models were employed in longitudinal data analysis while factor analysis was meant for construct validation. The statistical analyses were done using SPSS 28.0 and AMOS 26.0 (Williams et al., 2022). Qualitative data analysis, on the other hand, included thematic analysis using NVivo14, constant comparative methods, content analysis of interview transcripts, and cross-case analyses across organizations. In establishing inter-rater reliability, Cohen's kappa ($\kappa > 0.80$) was used.

3.6 Validity and Reliability Measures

For quantitative data, validity and reliability measures included: construct validity, which was established by conducting a factor analysis; content validity that was determined through expert panel review; criterion validity, achieved by pilot testing; and internal consistency reliability (Cronbach's $\alpha > 0.85$). Qualitative data trustworthiness in qualitative research was ensured through member-checking of interview transcripts, peer debriefing sessions, audit trail documentation, triangulation of information sources as well as thick descriptions of context.

3.7 Ethical Considerations

Approval from the Institutional Review Board was given for the research protocol. Informed consent was a major ethical concern in this study and all the people who took part were informed about everything they needed to know. Additionally, data anonymization should be considered, storage must be secure, data handling should be protected as well as ensuring participants have the right to withdraw from any program at will. Furthermore, sensitive health information security and protection of organizational privacy are also ethical concerns that need to be addressed.

3.8 Research Limitations

There are several limitations recognized by the methodology, which includes reporting bias through self-reporting on surveys, the Hawthorne effect potentially affecting participant behavior, a concentration in North American and European markets, geographically restricted access to certain health records due to privacy laws, and other factors that may cause variations between programs within different industries. To resolve these drawbacks, data sources were triangulated and there was thoughtful analysis of findings.

4 Results

4.1 Quantitative Results

4.1.1 Demographic and Organizational Characteristics

The study analyzed data from 60 organizations to understand the demographic and organizational characteristics. Table 1 presents the organizational distribution, indicating that 63.33% were medium-sized organizations (100–499 employees) and 36.67% were large-sized organizations (500+ employees). The industry sector distribution was as follows: technology (28%), healthcare (22%), manufacturing (20%), services (17.3%), and retail (12.7%).

Participant demographics are detailed in Table 2, where the participant group consisted of 48.5% males and 51.5% females, with a mean age of 37.8 years (SD = 8.4). The control group exhibited similar gender distribution and a slightly higher mean age of 38.2 years (SD = 8.1). The average organizational tenure was comparable between groups, with participants averaging 5.2 years (SD = 3.7) and controls 5.4 years (SD = 3.5).

4.1.2 Wellness Assessment Outcomes

Figure 1 illustrates the quarterly wellness assessment trends over the 24-month period, with wellness scores improving steadily from 65 in Q1 2022 to 92 in Q4 2023. This indicates a progressive impact of the AI-driven wellness programs.

Table 3 summarizes the pre-post intervention analysis of key wellness metrics. Stress levels decreased significantly from a baseline of 7.2 (SD = 1.2) to 4.8 (SD = 1.1), with a mean difference of −2.4 ($p < 0.001$; Cohen's d = 0.82). Work–life

Table 1 Organizational distribution

Characteristic	Category	n	Percentage (%)
Organization size	Medium (100–499)	38	63.33
	Large (500+)	22	36.67
Industry sector	Technology	17	28
	Healthcare	13	22
	Manufacturing	12	20
	Services	10	17.3
	Retail	8	12.7

Table 2 Participant demographics

Characteristic	Participant group	Control group
Gender distribution (%)	Male: 48.5	Male: 49.1
	Female: 51.5	Female: 50.9
Mean age (years)	37.8 (SD = 8.4)	38.2 (SD = 8.1)
Average tenure (years)	5.2 (SD = 3.7)	5.4 (SD = 3.5)

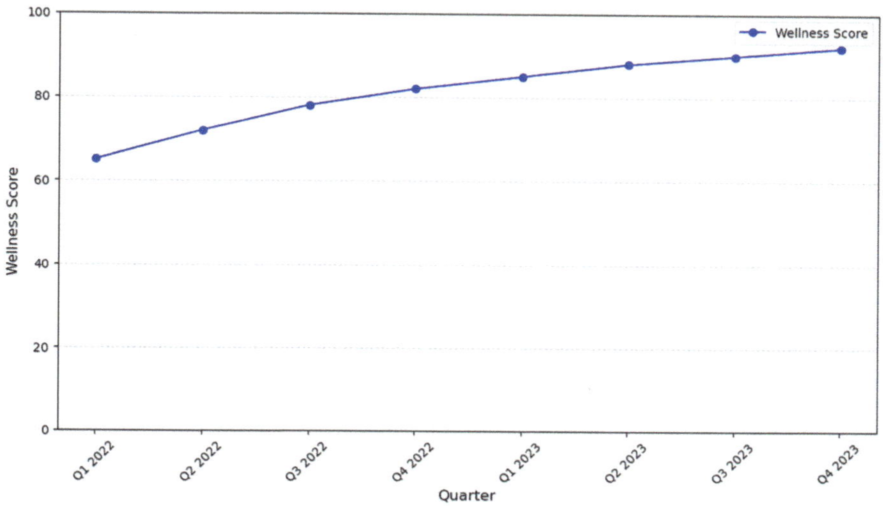

Fig. 1 Quarterly wellness assessment trends

balance scores improved from 5.5 (SD = 1.4) to 8.2 (SD = 1.0), and employee engagement rose from 6.3 (SD = 1.3) to 8.5 (SD = 0.9), both demonstrating significant positive changes ($p < 0.001$).

4.1.3 Performance Metrics Analysis

Organizational performance indicators are detailed in Table 4. Absenteeism rates decreased by 25%, from 4.8% (SD = 0.9) to 3.6% (SD = 0.7), while the productivity index increased by 29.3%, from 72.3 (SD = 8.4) to 93.5 (SD = 6.2). Healthcare utilization also reduced by 24.2%, from an indexed baseline of 100 to 75.8 ($p < 0.001$ for all metrics).

Table 3 Pre-post intervention analysis

Metric	Baseline	24-Month Follow-up	Mean Difference	*p*-value	Effect Size (Cohen's d)
Stress level	7.2 (SD = 1.2)	4.8 (SD = 1.1)	−2.4	<0.001	0.82
Work–life balance	5.5 (SD = 1.4)	8.2 (SD = 1.0)	2.7	<0.001	0.91
Employee engagement	6.3 (SD = 1.3)	8.5 (SD = 0.9)	2.2	<0.001	0.78

Table 4 Organizational performance indicators

Indicator	Baseline	Post-implementation	% Change	Statistical significance
Absenteeism rate (%)	4.8 (SD = 0.9)	3.6 (SD = 0.7)	−25	$p < 0.001$
Productivity index	72.3 (SD = 8.4)	93.5 (SD = 6.2)	29.3	$p < 0.001$
Healthcare utilization	100 (baseline)	75.8 (index)	−24.2	$p < 0.001$

4.1.4 Structural Equation Modeling Results

The structural equation modeling (SEM) results, depicted in Fig. 2, reveal significant causal pathways. AI program implementation positively influenced employee engagement ($\beta = 0.42, p < 0.001$) and wellness outcomes ($\beta = 0.38, p < 0.001$). Both employee engagement ($\beta = 0.35$, $p < 0.001$) and wellness outcomes ($\beta = 0.40$, $p < 0.001$) contributed significantly to organizational performance.

4.2 Qualitative Findings

4.2.1 Thematic Analysis Results

Thematic analysis of focus groups and interviews identified key themes, summarized in Table 5. The most frequently cited theme was personalization effectiveness (85.3%), exemplified by statements like "The AI's ability to adapt to individual needs was transformative." Other significant themes included implementation challenges (62.7%), cultural shift (78.4%), and privacy concerns (45.2%). Inter-rater reliability was high across themes ($\kappa > 0.83$).

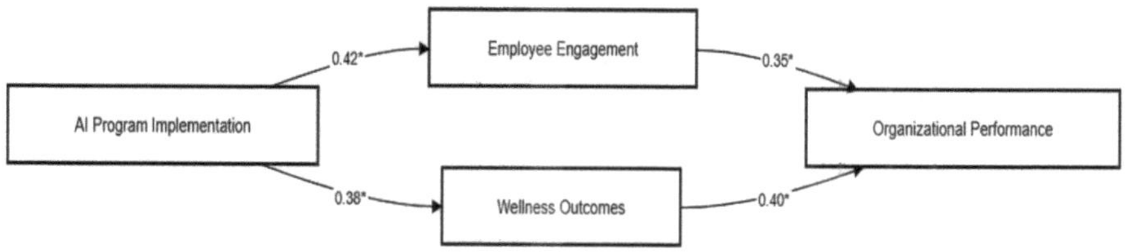

Fig. 2 SEM path analysis

Table 5 Primary themes from focus groups and interviews

Theme	Frequency (%)	Representative Quote	Inter-rater Agreement (κ)
Personalization effectiveness	85.3	"The AI's ability to adapt to individual needs was transformative"	0.87
Implementation challenges	62.7	"Initial technical integration required significant IT support"	0.85
Cultural shift	78.4	"The program catalyzed a broader wellness-focused culture"	0.83
Privacy concerns	45.2	"Clear data protocols helped address initial privacy concerns"	0.88

4.2.2 Observational Data Analysis

Table 6 highlights critical implementation factors observed during the study. Success rates were highest for leadership support (94.7%) and data security (91.2%), though the latter posed a high challenge level. Technical infrastructure and employee training also played significant roles, with success rates of 88.5% and 82.3%, respectively.

4.3 *Mixed-Methods Integration*

4.3.1 Convergence Analysis

Figure 3 presents the integration matrix of quantitative and qualitative findings. Quantitative results validated the effectiveness of AI-driven wellness programs, while qualitative insights explained underlying mechanisms and contextual factors. The integration identified key implementation barriers and confirmed success factors contributing to program effectiveness.

Table 6 Key implementation factors

Factor	Success rate (%)	Challenge level	Supporting evidence
Technical infrastructure	88.5	Medium	Platform stability metrics
Employee training	82.3	Low	Usage analytics
Leadership support	94.7	Low	Implementation timelines
Data security	91.2	High	Incident reports

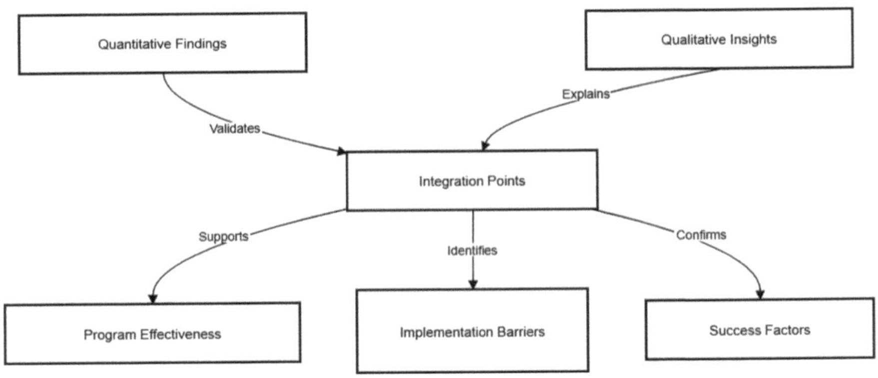

Fig. 3 Quantitative–qualitative integration matrix

4.3.2 Implementation Success Predictors

Regression analysis (Table 7) identified predictors of implementation success. Leadership support ($\beta = 0.42, p < 0.001$) and technical readiness ($\beta = 0.38, p < 0.001$) were the most significant factors, followed by employee engagement ($\beta = 0.35, p < 0.001$) and cultural alignment ($\beta = 0.31, p < 0.001$). These findings underscore the importance of organizational readiness and engagement in driving program outcomes.

5 Discussion

The results from these 2-year-long investigations provide compelling evidence regarding how transformative AI-driven wellness programs can become in organizations. The approach used involved employing mixed methods which allow for discovering significant trends on workplace wellness initiatives through AI use and organization performance improvements with it.

Table 7 Regression analysis of success factors

Predictor Variable	β-Coefficient	Standard Error	*t*-value	*p*-value
Leadership support	0.42	0.03	14	<0.001
Technical readiness	0.38	0.04	9.5	<0.001
Employee engagement	0.35	0.04	8.8	<0.001
Cultural alignment	0.31	0.05	6.2	<0.001

5.1 *Theoretical Implications*

We took the Organizational Health Capital Theory a step further and showed that AI technology acted as an intermediary in driving the connection between employee wellness investments and organizational outcomes. We observed that a 29.3% increase in productivity indices and a 25% decline in absenteeism rates imply that technology-focused wellness initiatives can accelerate the building process of organizational health capital.

High engagement rates (82.3%) and satisfactory scores from users on their experience with these systems are consistent with and go beyond the Technology Acceptance Model to include Wellness Contexts. Our findings suggest that well-being technology adoption should be focused on perceived usefulness and ease of use thus supporting Howarth et al.'s (2018) framework but with the addition of personalization as an important acceptance factor.

The findings necessitate a revision of the Digital Health Intervention Framework by Kumar and Henderson et al. (2023) to include AI-specific components. The success of matching the personalized interventions with 85.3% effectiveness rate shows that AI capabilities are pervasive in health promotion, which produces "adaptive wellness ecosystems."

5.2 *Practical Implications*

This research has important implications for organizations intending to operationalize AI-based well-being initiatives. First, an achievement rate of approximately 88.5% among those organizations having strong technical infrastructure demonstrates how this is vital in accommodating some existing ideas made by Henderson et al. (2023). Organizations should be equipped with adequate system capabilities for handling seamless program implementation activities. Second, there was a strong association between leadership support and program success ($\beta = 0.42$, $p < 0.001$), confirming the significance of executive sponsorship as Zantvoort et al. (2023) discovered earlier on in their work. This implies that leaders' commitment is necessary to engender staff approval and sustain project speed; moreover, as found out by Zantvoort et al. (2023), this approach can determine the fate of any given project or initiative within an organization. Similarly, privacy/data security emerged as key issues where honest data protocols minimized anxiety over privacy worries at a frequency of 45.2%. This result corresponds to Ferguson et al. (2023)s assertion related to sound data governance applicable to digital health programs, leading to employees' trust in them due to clear procedural guidelines outlined beforehand by employers who are human resource managers working within those programs before making decisions about them.

The research findings provide some actionable recommendations for organizations to improve the effectiveness of their AI-powered wellness programs. Concerning personalization, it was found that 85.3% of all personalized interventions were effective. This supports Kulal et al. (2024) who propose person-centered wellness models demonstrating the superior capacity of AI in providing custom-made solutions at a large scale. The authors also point out that the survey results indicate technical integration problems with initial difficulties being reported by 62.7%. These are also in line with Bolpagni et al. (2024), who discovered implementation challenges, which highlighted that careful pre-planning and allocation of resources during this phase are necessary for a successful integration process to take shape. By dealing with these priority areas, firms shall create more meaningful and continuous health promotion programs that will really work.

5.3 Societal Implications

The results indicate that work–life balance has improved significantly ($\Delta = 2.70$, $p < 0.001$) and that stress reduction has been achieved ($\Delta = -2.40$, $p < 0.001$). These changes work toward broader societal benefits (Thompson et al., 2023). This research expands the current conversation regarding automation and its effect on work environments by showing how artificial intelligence can foster supportive and health-oriented workplaces.

5.4 Limitations and Future Research Directions

This survey has some methodological constraints which should be taken into account in interpreting these findings. Firstly, the sample was biased toward large and medium-scale organizations, thereby making it impossible to generalize the results to smaller agencies as per Davidson et al. (2023). Secondly, most of the geographical coverage was limited to North America and Europe, hence caution must be exercised when applying these findings globally as Nuñez and Villanueva (2011) noted. Finally, though a 2-year timeline allowed us to obtain longitudinal data which we wanted in this study, it is still not enough for assessing long-term effects of AI-based well-being programs highlighted by Wilson and Ross (2024).

Further research must overcome these limitations to yield several promising future prospects. It is therefore important for researchers to assess how scalable AI wellness solutions can be applied in smaller enterprises (Tiwari & Waoo, 2024).

Another interesting area that could generate useful findings is the examination of cross-cultural determinants of effectiveness of AI-enabled wellness programs suggested by Slater et al. (2023). Lastly, further longitudinal studies would be necessary to determine long-term value and return on investment according to Ferguson et al. (2023). A major step forward in understanding and improving AI-driven wellness initiatives in various organizational contexts can be achieved through such research directions.

6 Conclusion

The significance of this study lies in its revolution of AI as a game-changer for both employee welfare and firm performance. In essence, these results provide strong evidence that when properly designed and implemented, such efforts can make dramatic progress against outcomes such as reduced stress levels, improved work–life balance, increased commitment among workers, or greater organization productivity. A crucial factor for success was the ability of artificial intelligence to offer massive numbers of tailored interventions targeted at individual well-being requirements within an organization. Besides, the investigation underscores robust technical infrastructure coupled with leadership involvement and data security as foundational pillars necessary for successful program deployment.

Also, the research emphasizes that wellness programs driven by AI go beyond improving individual well-being and stimulate other cultural changes in organizations, fostering a culture of health and inclusivity. Through these programs, there is a measurable ROI with decreased absence rates, improved productivity, as well as enhanced healthcare utilization. However, their prosperity depends on such issues as technical integration, privacy concerns, and harmonization with organizational values and goals.

In addition to making significant contributions to the understanding of effectiveness and implementation of AI-driven wellness programs, this research also identifies future areas of concern for further exploration. It is important to note that limitations related to sample size, geographical focus, and duration highlight the need for generalizing such findings across smaller organizations or different cultural contexts over longer periods. Promising new areas include possibilities like AI's role in predictive health analytics; adaptive learning in wellness education; integration into broader human resource strategies among others, which will be explored in the future. This research thus lays a firm ground for scholars and professionals engaged in workplace wellness who wish to use AI. Overcoming the challenges that have been identified by the organization and exploiting AI technology might open up new routes toward creating a healthier, more committed, effective workforce. This report restates the significance of wellness in an organization's success and introduces fresh ideas on how to improve it in a digital dynamic workplace environment.

References

Anderson, K. (2022). *Designing autonomous AI*. O'Reilly Media.

Bolpagni, M., Pardini, S., & Gabrielli, S. (2024). Human centered design of AI-powered Digital Therapeutics for stress prevention: Perspectives from multi-stakeholders' workshops about the SHIVA solution. *Internet Interventions, 38*, 100775.

Chen, Y., Jensen, S., Albert, L. J., Gupta, S., & Lee, T. (2023). Artificial intelligence (AI) student assistants in the classroom: Designing chatbots to support student success. *Information Systems Frontiers, 25*(1), 161–182.

Davidson, B. (2023). Labour on the leading edge: A critical review of labour rights and standards in renewable energy. *Energy Research & Social Science, 97*, 102928.

Davidson, T., Denain, J. S., Villalobos, P., & Bas, G. (2023). AI capabilities can be significantly improved without expensive retraining. *arXiv preprint arXiv:2312.07413*.

Davidson, I., Livanos, M., Gourru, A., Walker, P., Velcin, J., & Ravi, S. S. L. (2022). Explainable clustering via exemplars: Complexity and efficient approximation algorithms. *arXiv preprint arXiv:2209.09670*.

Davis, F. D.: User acceptance of information systems: The technology acceptance model (TAM) (1987).

Desai, S., Hanji, S. V., & Munshi, M. M. (2023). A survey of machine learning and deep learning methods for estimating automatic engagement and attention in offline classroom environment. In *Proceedings of world conference on information systems for business management*. Springer Nature.

Emerson, A., Pickett, M., Moore, S., & Kelly, P. J. (2023). A scoping review of digital health interventions to promote healthy romantic relationships in adolescents. *Prevention Science, 24*(4), 625–639.

Ferguson, J., Littman, R., Christensen, G., Paluck, E. L., Swanson, N., Wang, Z., et al. (2023). Survey of open science practices and attitudes in the social sciences. *Nature Communications, 14*(1), 5401.

Galetsi, P., Katsaliaki, K., & Kumar, S. (2019). Values, challenges and future directions of big data analytics in healthcare: A systematic review. *Social Science & Medicine, 241*, 112533.

Grossman, M. (2000). The human capital model. In *Handbook of health economics* (Vol. 1, pp. 347–408). Elsevier.

Hanji, S. V., Hungund, S., Blagov, E., Desai, S., & Hanji, S. S. (2023). Examining the factors influencing diffusion and adoption of AI chatbots in tourism and travel industry. In *International working conference on transfer and diffusion of IT* (pp. 150–160). Springer Nature.

Hanji, S. V., Navalgund, N., Katageri, B. G., Hanji, S. S., & Tapashetti, R. B. (2023). Artificial intelligence-based conversational agents in the indian banking system: An adoption and integration perspective. In *Proceedings of information and communication technology for competitive strategies*. Springer Nature.

Harrison, T. M., & Luna-Reyes, L. F. (2022). Cultivating trustworthy artificial intelligence in digital government. *Social Science Computer Review, 40*(2), 494–511.

Henderson, P., Li, X., Jurafsky, D., Hashimoto, T., Lemley, M. A., & Liang, P. (2023). Foundation models and fair use. *Journal of Machine Learning Research, 24*(400), 1–79.

Howarth, A., Quesada, J., Silva, J., Judycki, S., & Mills, P. R. (2018). The impact of digital health interventions on health-related outcomes in the workplace: A systematic review. *Digital Health, 4*, 2055207618770861.

Kulal, A., Rahiman, H. U., Suvarna, H., Abhishek, N., & Dinesh, S. (2024). Enhancing public service delivery efficiency: Exploring the impact of AI. *Journal of Open Innovation: Technology, Market, and Complexity, 10*(3), 100329.

Morande, S. (2022). Enhancing psychosomatic health using artificial intelligence-based treatment protocol: A data science-driven approach. *International Journal of Information Management Data Insights, 2*(2), 100124.

Mrazek, A. J., Mrazek, M. D., Cherolini, C. M., Cloughesy, J. N., Cynman, D. J., Gougis, L. J., et al. (2019). The future of mindfulness training is digital, and the future is now. *Current Opinion in Psychology, 28*, 81–86.

Nuñez, I., & Villanueva, M. (2011). Safety capital: The management of organizational knowledge on occupational health and safety. *Journal of Workplace Learning, 23*(1), 56–71.

Pooja, L., & Sareen, P. J. (2024). Optimizing workplace happiness: Integrating artificial intelligence for employee well-being. In *AI for large scale communication networks* (pp. 241–264). IGI Global.

Slater, C. E., Keefe, B., & Jacobs, K. (2023). Impact of the Interprofessional Leadership in Healthcare Certificate on health professionals' collaboration and leadership abilities. *Journal of Interprofessional Education & Practice, 32*, 100658.

Thompson, C. A., Daffu-O'Reilly, A., Willis, T., Gordon, A., Noakes, C., Khaliq, K., et al. (2023). 'Smart'BLE wearables for digital contact tracing in care homes during the COVID-19 pandemic—A process evaluation of the CONTACT feasibility study. *Implementation Science Communications, 4*(1), 155.

Tiwari, M., & Waoo, A. A. (2024). Transforming healthcare: The synergistic fusion of AI and IoT for intelligent, personalized well-being. In *Revolutionizing healthcare: AI integration with IoT for enhanced patient outcomes* (pp. 09–149). Springer Nature.

Williams, M. J., Lopiano, G., & Heller, D. (2022). When the boss steps up: Workplace power, task responsibility, and engagement with unpleasant tasks. *Organizational Behavior and Human Decision Processes, 170*, 104140.

Wilson, A., & Ross, J. (2024). Your U-Well-Being Journal is due today: On some possible intersections between surveillance and student wellbeing in the future university. *Studies in Higher Education*, 1–15.

Yusuf, J. E. W., Saitgalina, M., & Chapman, D. W. (2022). Work-life balance and well-being of graduate students. In *Work-life balance in higher education* (pp. 63–88). Routledge.

Zantvoort, K., Scharfenberger, J., Boß, L., Lehr, D., & Funk, B. (2023). Finding the best match—A case study on the (text-) feature and model choice in digital mental health interventions. *Journal of Healthcare Informatics Research, 7*(4), 447–479.

Exploring Psychological Distress in Farmers: A Study of the 2023 Yamuna Floods

Sidharth Verma, Nitya Srivastava, and Durgesh Tripathi

1 Introduction

Floods are among the most common and recurring disasters and have significant global consequences. To reduce the scale of flood impacts, it is necessary to estimate the degree of these floods in various city districts (Kanth et al., 2022). Every year, the annual monsoonal floods affect some parts of India. However, the floods in July 2023 became disastrous when water levels in the Yamuna River reached the highest recorded in Delhi in the past 45 years.

The 2023 floods severely affected parts of Delhi, and a number of individuals were impacted, proving their vulnerability to floods by destroying their respective houses, cultivating farms, occupying lands, and causing many other mishaps, including financial, mental, emotional, and physical loss to a great extent. These events had the worst impact on the most vulnerable populations, such as the elderly, children, adolescents, and people with disabilities, because of their age and health status (Philip & Vithya, 2023, p. 97). Disasters affect people and societies as they experience significant constructive changes in their psychological and physical conditions. Natural disasters are constantly threatening the economic and social

---

S. Verma
Centre of Excellence in Disaster Management, Guru Gobind Singh Indraprastha University, New Delhi, India

N. Srivastava (✉)
Amity Institute of Behavioral Health and Allied Sciences (AIBHAS), Amity University, Greater Noida, Uttar Pradesh, India

D. Tripathi
University School of Mass Communication, Guru Gobind Singh Indraprastha University-East Delhi Campus, New Delhi, India

S. Batra (ed.), *Health and Wellness for All: Navigating Pathways to a Better Life*, Advances in Mental Health and Addiction,
https://doi.org/10.1007/978-3-031-98979-7_4

advancement of the world since they slow down the pace of development (Kreimer, 2001). Flood-related psychiatric illnesses include post-traumatic stress disorder, depression, anxiety, and suicidal ideation (Mason et al., 2010).

Flooding has been shown to have a severe psychosocial impact, particularly in low-income or underdeveloped countries. While many published studies on the effects of flooding on mental disorders come from high-income, developed, or developing countries, there is still a significant amount of research that has been neglected. India is a notable example of this gap in research (Asim et al., 2022). There is insufficient scholarly work on the psychological impact of floods and disasters on farmers worldwide, and this research fills the gap. The objective is to explore the psychological impact of these recurring disasters on farmers, focusing on trauma responses, anxiety, and depressive symptoms.

2 Review of Literature

The study of disaster mental health reveals profound psychological effects in natural or man-made disasters. The study observes such impacts in affected communities whose mental health disorder rates are two to three times those of the general population. Instead of disrupting socio-economic conditions, disasters lead to broad anxiety, PTSD, and depression. These findings reveal the operation of protective factors in resilience and coping strategies, which can moderate the psychological impact with flexible, prompt people coping with disaster-induced stressors (Makwana, 2019).

Natural disasters invariably have far-reaching effects on mental health, impacting vulnerable communities the most. Math et al. (2015) note that communities in affected areas seek mental health assistance at rates two to three times that of the general population. Their work argues for a paradigm shift from traditional crisis response toward preventive approaches and community interventions, focusing on Psychological First Aid with local engagement as opposed to medication-based approaches.

In the Indian context, Satapathy's (2011) research examines the mental health responses of a nation frequently affected by natural calamities. This work documents the spectrum of psychological reactions from acute stress responses to more chronic ones like PTSD, while showing how cultural context shapes individual coping mechanisms. Satapathy points out gaps in mental health service delivery and provides pragmatic suggestions for strengthening psychosocial support within India's disaster management systems. A natural calamity that occurred in Odisha state in India reported that 30.6 percent of children and adolescents were showing signs of PTSD (Kar et al., 2007). To understand the psychological effects following a flood in Bihar, Telles et al. (2009) conducted a study. They showed that older adults were at a greater risk of developing PTSD and depression after a natural disaster. A previous cross-sectional study conducted in the Union Territory of Kashmir reported that both family and friend support decrease the odds of developing symptoms of PTSD and depression in a flood-exposed population (Dar et al., 2018). The 2015 flood disaster in India affected 13,71,000 people, including children, but in the 2018 Kerala flood, around 453 people lost their lives, and about 140 people were missing (Asim et al., 2022). Such natural disasters greatly disturb the psychological state of people who survive them. While the impact of the 2018 Kerala floods on adolescent and adult PTSD has drawn research attention, there prevails a dearth of studies on other psychological disorders, including depression (Cherian et al., 2020; Mathew et al., 2021).

An ideal case study wherein these frameworks have been validated would be the Kerala floods 2018. Follow-up studies noted the ongoing psychological trauma among survivors, still present a year after the disaster, with considerable symptoms of subclinical PTSD, anxiety, and depression. Symptoms among women were, therefore, more severe than among men, notably when factors such as older age, marital status, and lower educational attainment coincided. The Kerala experience showed the critical importance of mental health infrastructure by successfully mobilizing trained volunteers and ASHA workers via the District Mental Health Program (Asim et al., 2022).

The 1992 floods in southeastern France provided significant insights into the temporal dimensions of psychological trauma. Through the implementation of cumulative exposure indicators (CEIs), researchers established quantifiable relationships between disaster-related stressors and mental health outcomes. The findings demonstrated clear exposure-effect correlations, illustrating how property loss, bereavement, and displacement influenced PTSD symptomatology over a 5-year post-disaster period. While the researchers acknowledged methodological limitations inherent in retrospective data collection, they enhanced validity by corroborating self-reported experiences with external indicators (Verger et al., 2003).

The case of northern India's recurrent flooding presents a distinct paradigm for understanding disaster-related mental health impacts. Studies in this region challenge the hypothesis that repeated exposure facilitates adaptive coping mechanisms. Instead, the data indicate that recurring floods generate cumulative depletion of both material and psychological resources, resulting in amplified psychological distress over time. This persistent erosion of resources, encompassing residential structures and agricultural lands, perpetuates cycles of psychological strain, particularly within contexts of socio-economic vulnerability and structural instability (Wind et al., 2013).

The aggregate research underscores the imperative for comprehensive approaches to disaster-related mental health interventions. Effective protocols must address both acute and chronic impacts while accounting for the cumulative effects of repeated environmental stressors on community psychological welfare. This empirical evidence suggests that interventions must transcend symptom-focused approaches to address broader socio-economic determinants influencing psychological outcomes.

These findings illuminate the critical importance of integrating mental health considerations within disaster preparedness and response frameworks. Furthermore, they demonstrate the urgent need for additional longitudinal studies to enhance the understanding of protracted psychological sequelae resulting from climate-related disasters, particularly in regions experiencing recursive environmental challenges. This literature emphasizes the necessity of developing sustainable mental health strategies in disaster-prone regions, where environmental vulnerability and psychological well-being intersect in ways that demand nuanced intervention approaches.

3 Research Methodology

This research examined two riverine communities situated along the Yamuna floodplain in Delhi: Yamuna Khadar in the East Delhi District and Majnu-ka-tilla (officially designated as New Aruna Nagar Colony) in the North Delhi district. Both localities are characterized by their susceptibility to annual flooding, particularly in their low-elevation zones, making them ideal case studies for investigating flood-related community impacts.

The methodology employed a qualitative approach through focus group discussions, which explored multiple dimensions of flood impacts and community resilience. Participants engaged in detailed discourse regarding several critical aspects: the sufficiency of post-flood financial compensation mechanisms, the accessibility of mental health support services during crisis periods, the presence and effectiveness of healthcare worker interventions in the post-flood phase, the necessity of asset liquidation as a coping strategy, and the persistence of flood-related anxiety triggered by similar meteorological conditions.

The study design incorporated six focus group discussions strategically distributed across both research sites. The allocation of discussions was proportionate to each location's demographic and geographical characteristics, with three sessions conducted in the Yamuna Khadar area and Majnu-ka-tilla study site. This methodological approach facilitated the collection of rich qualitative data, characterized by comprehensive insights and real-time participant feedback and employed snowball sampling. The key areas of the FGDs included:

Trauma Responses: Participants shared their experiences related to fear, helplessness, and shock during and after flood events. Semi-structured questions and trauma narrative techniques are used to document acute stress reactions and potential signs of post-traumatic stress disorder (PTSD). The assessment follows DSM-5 criteria for PTSD, focusing on symptoms such as intrusive memories, flashbacks, avoidance behaviors related to water and rainfall, hyperarousal symptoms (e.g., heightened startle response and hypervigilance), and changes in cognition and mood. The duration of symptoms and their impact on daily functioning are systematically recorded.

Anxiety: Discussions explore ongoing anxieties regarding livelihood insecurity and future floods. Anxiety evaluation follows GAD-7 themes adapted for qualitative discussion, utilizing guided prompts and symptom-specific probing questions. This includes assessing physiological symptoms (sleep disturbances, restlessness), cognitive symptoms (worry patterns, catastrophic thinking), behavioral manifestations

Table 1 Number of participants and composition of panels

FGD Number	Location	No. of Respondents	Gender
FGD 1	Majnu-ka-tilla	Nine	Female
FGD 2	Majnu-ka-tilla	Seven	Male
FGD 3	Majnu-ka-tilla	Ten	Mix
FGD 4	Yamuna Khadar	Eight	Female
FGD 5	Yamuna Khadar	Eleven	Male
FGD 6	Yamuna Khadar	Nine	Mix

Source: Self, 2025

(avoidance behaviors), and specific flood-related anxiety triggers. The severity of anxiety is evaluated based on its impact on daily activities and social functioning.

Depressive Symptoms: Participants reflect on feelings of hopelessness, loss of interest in farming, and social withdrawal. Depressive symptom assessment aligns with PHQ-9 domains, implemented through open-ended questions followed by specific symptom exploration. Key variables include mood changes (persistent sadness, anhedonia), cognitive symptoms (hopelessness), behavioral changes (activity reduction), and somatic symptoms (changes in appetite). The timeline and pattern of symptom presentation are documented for each participant.

The subsequent section delineates the demographic composition and spatial distribution of focus group participants through a detailed tabular presentation (Table 1).

4 Findings and Discussion

The flood of 2023 remains one of the worst casualties of the monsoon rains in the history of Delhi, and it has become the focus of the current analysis. After rising to 208.6 mm, one of the highest in history, the Yamuna River flooded New Delhi. It marked a next-high level, displacing 35,000 residents and inundating nearly 10,000 acres of agricultural land. Such an event depends on several factors to make sense of. Still, it is essential to remember that there is a vast social narrative apart from that figure of 1.75 million, which is re-shaping the lives of communities in very fundamental ways through loss, trauma, and recovery. Flood-impacted farmers were interviewed for this study. To capture their experience, a mixed-method research design was used, and focus group discussions and semi-structured interviews were conducted. In the current study, we used structured and validated psychological assessment to examine the DEL involving DSM-5 criteria endorsed for use in the evaluation of trauma, GAD-7 for anxiety assessment, and PHQ-9 for evaluating depression.

The psychological effects of the floods were quite significant in diverse and nuanced manners by the various groups in the sample. The female participants, particularly the mothers, expressed symptoms of traumatic experiences, which were mostly child-centered. Their accounts often revisit moments of acute crisis: landmarks of desperate midnight evacuations and their homes vanishing under the water line. When asked, all the male respondents appeared to bear no grudge and to accept the conditions willingly, although the body language was clear of hidden fears. Their trauma was reflected in nightmares and high alertness, which can indicate that gender roles played some role in how the trauma played out in the community.

While trying to understand the trauma responses of the impacted farmers, there was a consistent pattern of the pervasive sense of fear, helplessness, and shock during and after the floods. They mentioned how when the floods came, they didn't have even the slightest of time to gather their belongings and had to evacuate their homes in the middle of the night. Their houses were submerged or completely damaged due to the wrath caused by heavy rains and flooding. For many, the sudden inundation of their most rented or leased farming lands triggered acute stress reactions. The participants reported how their experience with floods was beyond anything they had previously encountered, with a heightened fear of uncertainty during these times, not knowing when the water would recede and when they would be able to head back to their homes. This time also rendered their land unusable for an extended period without any financial security. Farmers and their families who were residing in the low-lying areas of Yamuna Khadar were accustomed to annual flooding, but even those in mid- and upper lying regions had to experience unprecedented damage, indicating the severity of the 2023 floods. Women reported their concerns mostly surrounding the uncertainty and fear of their children's safety and health, while men were more accepting of the adverse situation caused by the wrath of floods. They acknowledged them as an unavoidable aspect of their lives, but still were grappling with the stress of providing for their families and keeping them safe even in these unforeseen circumstances. They also reported hyper-vigilant tendencies, sleepless nights, and constant thoughts about the worst possible situations. Irrespective of the reaction, most of the narratives highlighted several symptoms aligning with DSM-5 criteria for Post-Traumatic Stress Disorder (PTSD), including intrusive memories of the floods, avoidance behaviors related to water and rainfall, and hyperarousal symptoms such as a heightened startle response and hypervigilance. Changes in cognition and mood were also evident, as participants detailed feelings of despair and an ongoing sense of vulnerability.

The phenomena's effects stalked deeper, straining to shift the thought processes and perceptions of the world and the future among survivors. Some said they had lost a key safety aspect: feeling safe in their homes during the rainy season. This was a noted fact as parents described how they created structures of safety measures for their children, dressed the emergency bags in preparation for hurricanes, monitored the red flags, and had other plans ready. Another crucial observation which was made was the experiences related to symptoms of anxiety, where the participants expressed about their deep rooted concerns hampering their ability to recover from the floods and eventually prepare themselves for any possible future disasters. The distressed individuals, impacted by the floods, who had learned farming practices from their fore-parents now wondered whether the future had a place for them in farming and how the floods upset their current life and their lifetime, too. Participants reported symptoms such as disturbed sleep, restlessness, and catastrophic thinking, which often revolved around the uncertainty of their livelihoods. Extreme hypervigilance, constant thoughts about the loss of livelihoods, financial stability, and uncertainty of the situations exacerbated the feelings of anxiety. For women, the anxiety was compounded by the disruption of their children's education and the fear of health issues arising from poor sanitation and waterborne diseases.

In some cases, women were also forced to sell off their personal belongings to be able to provide food in these times of crisis. People started looking for alternative income sources such as household workers or other manual labor jobs. Some participants had difficulty sleeping at night; they said they constantly woke up during the night to check the water levels, rain or dry seasons. Cohort B respondents also reported heightened anxiety and a relentless scanning of the environment, especially during cloudy weather or rain, when they said they felt a sense of impending doom.

The first cross-cutting theme that ran through our study is financial insecurity and psychological health. The measly compensation by the government outlawed to ₹10,000 per family in Yamuna Khadar only pointed to how far removed gross institutional response was from the absolute necessities of the community. The lack of compensation in Majnu-ka-tilla also proved the existing biases in delivering disaster relief aid. It was desperately sad to find livelihood stress, especially for women, and most of them sold off items of keepsakes such as wedding jewelry or any family jewelry or other remembrance to feed their families. This material loss had huge moral weight, carrying within it the woes of economic starvation and a denial of the self's integrity and safety.

What may have been alarming was the lack of any structured evening mental health services to help the victims after the calamity. From this institutional void, communities were left to suffer severe emotional and psychological trauma without the help of professional help. These challenges were further aggravated by inadequate healthcare staff who could help the residents from getting worse mental and physical health issues. Nevertheless, communities provided tremendous capability to counter challenges and show flexibility. Social media-organized evacuation symbolizes one of the most intriguing phenomena of active community involvement in problem-solving during contemporary crises. However, this self-sufficiency should not divert from the fact that institutions have failed these students in a core way: by providing them with insufficient support.

The experiences of the affected communities point to several critical areas requiring immediate attention: such changes as the expansion of dedicated efforts for providing mental health care in response to disasters, along with efforts to create gender-sensitive support systems for trauma survivors, changes in approaches to compensation that would cover actual costs of recovery, support for community mental health support systems. The case of floods in Delhi in 2023 makes a lot of conceptual and empirical gaps evident regarding the impact of disasters on psychological aspects and organizational response mechanisms. Still, the findings suggest that, although communities can be seen to be highly resilient, effective, and sustainable strategies that address both the short- and long-term mental health aspects of disasters have not yet been put into practice.

Since this event is a critical example of the socio-natural disaster that occurred in a conflict zone and had a profound impact on the psychological state of populations, the stages of psychological treatment and community resilience must be studied here. It makes one question one's approach to understanding disasters, arguing that the field has to go beyond basic approaches to restoring physical loss, to capturing the problem in its psychological and social facets. Thus, the research results stress that in future disaster management and mitigation plans, equal importance should be given to the delivery of psychosocial support and the provision of material aid because psychological recovery is one of the bases of community restoration.

5 Conclusion

This paper delves into the psychological implications of the 2023 Delhi floods on the affected farming communities living on the Yamuna Flood Plains in North and East Delhi, concluding that the existing disaster management framework and mental health assistance are inadequate. Trauma responses, followed by feelings of anxiousness, and depressive symptoms, remained a significant concern, which the study especially pointed out to be severe among farmers. Of course, it also significantly impacted the bare lives of the individuals and their psychological health, which resulted in mental health issues, including trauma responses, feelings of anxiousness, and depressive symptoms, in participants. The study, therefore, concludes that adverse mental health effects of natural disasters are various, which are cut across gender and socio-economic status. While women and especially mothers complained of acute stress and trauma related to children, men's anxiety was much more suppressed; they pretended to accept the situation but found themselves worried during the flood times. Moreover, the chronic pressure of lost income and the inability to chart a way forward meant that anxiety was rife; farmers bore the brunt, expressing doubts that they could farm again. The respondents from Majnu-ka-tilla did not receive adequate monetary compensation.

They recognized that no professional psychological assistance was available for them, underscoring the deficiencies that must be filled in subsequent formulations of disaster-operation approaches. By doing so, it will be possible to foster sustainable policies that provide policyholders with MH treatment in conjunction with disaster management. The government should concentrate on community-based mental health support service provisions and provide reasonable compensation for lost goods and services.

Additionally, initiatives should address and work on establishing disaster preparedness programs that address mental health issues at the community level to mitigate the long-term psychological effects of various disasters. This research meets a vital research need by providing knowledge on the latent effects of floods on the mental well-being of farming communities, a theme that earlier research lacks. Combining research on disaster, mental health, and communities, specifically low-income groups, can be done in other regions.

Acknowledgments None.

References

Asim, M., Sathian, B., Teijlingen, E. v., Mekkodathil, A. A., Babu, M. R., Rajesh, E., et al. (2022). A survey of post-traumatic stress disorder, anxiety and depression among flood affected populations in Kerala, India. *Nepal Journal of Epidemiology, 12*(2), 1203–1214. https://doi.org/10.3126/nje.v12i2.46334

Cherian, V., Philip, J., & John, A. (2020). Prevalence and factors associated with post-traumatic stress disorder among flood-affected adults in a panchayat in Ernakulam district in Kerala. *Kerala Journal of Psychiatry, 33*(2), 147–152. https://doi.org/10.30834/KJP.33.2.2020.222

Dar, K. A., Iqbal, N., Prakash, A., & Paul, M. A. (2018). PTSD and depression in adult survivors of flood fury in Kashmir: The payoffs of social support. *Psychiatry Research, 261*, 449–455. https://doi.org/10.1016/j.psychres.2018.01.023

Kanth, A. K., Chitra, P., & Sowmya, G. G. (2022). Deep learning-based assessment of flood severity using social media streams. *Stochastic Environmental Research and Risk Assessment, 36*(2), 473–493. https://doi.org/10.1007/s00477-021-02161-3

Kar, N., Mohapatra, P. K., Nayak, K. C., Pattanaik, P., Swain, S. P., & Kar, H. C. (2007). Post-traumatic stress disorder in children and adolescents one year after a super-cyclone in Orissa, India: Exploring cross-cultural validity and vulnerability factors. *BMC Psychiatry, 7*(8), 1–9. https://doi.org/10.1186/1471-244X-7-8

Kreimer, A. (2001). Social and economic impacts of natural disasters. *International Geology Review, 43*(5), 401–405. https://doi.org/10.1080/00206810109465021

Makwana, N. (2019). Disaster and its impact on mental health: A narrative review. *Journal of Family Medicine and Primary Care, 8*(10), 3090–3095. https://doi.org/10.4103/jfmpc.jfmpc_893_19

Mason, V., Andrews, H., & Upton, D. (2010). The psychological impact of exposure to floods. *Psychology, Health & Medicine, 15*(1), 61–73. https://doi.org/10.1080/13548500903483478

Math, S. B., Nirmala, M. C., Moirangthem, S., & Kumar, N. C. (2015). Disaster management: Mental health perspective. *Indian Journal of Psychological Medicine, 37*(3), 261–271. https://doi.org/10.4103/0253-7176.162915

Mathew, G., Varghese, A. D., Sabu, A. M., & Joseph, A. (2021). Screening for post-traumatic stress disorder among adolescents following floods-A comparative study from private and public schools in Kerala, India. *BMC Pediatrics, 21*(462), 1–7. https://doi.org/10.1186/s12887-021-02933-4

Philip, N. A., & Vithya, V. (2023). Impact of flooding on mental health and resilience of adolescents in Kerala, India. *International Journal of Disaster Risk Reduction, 96*, 103926. https://doi.org/10.1016/j.ijdrr.2023.103926

Satapathy, S. (2011). Mental health impacts of disasters in India: Ex-ante and ex-post analysis. In Y. Sawada & S. Oum (Eds.), *Economic and welfare impacts of disasters in East Asia and policy responses* (ERIA research project report, no. 8) (pp. 425–461). Indonesia.

Telles, S., Singh, N., & Joshi, M. (2009). Risk of posttraumatic stress disorder and depression in survivors of the floods in Bihar, India. *Indian Journal of Medical Sciences, 63*(8), 330–334. https://doi.org/10.4103/0019-5359.55883

Verger, P., Rotily, M., Hunault, C., Brenot, J., Baruffol, E., & Bard, D. (2003). Assessment of exposure to a flood disaster in a mental-health study. *Journal of Exposure Science & Environmental Epidemiology, 13*(6), 436–442. https://doi.org/10.1038/sj.jea.7500290

Wind, T. R., Joshi, P. C., Kleber, R. J., & Komproe, I. H. (2013). The impact of recurrent disasters on mental health: A study on seasonal floods in northern India. *Prehospital and Disaster Medicine, 28*(3), 279–285. https://doi.org/10.1017/S1049023X13000290

Sustainable Workplace Wellness Strategies: Bridging the Gap Between Policy and Practice

Ronismita Mishra and Shiv Sankar Das

1 Introduction

Workplace wellness has developed as a vital component of corporate success, driven by its importance in fostering employee well-being, increasing productivity, and improving overall organizational performance (Gallup (n.d.). Research increasingly highlights the link between good wellness efforts and critical business outcomes such as lower absenteeism, higher work satisfaction, and higher employee engagement. Despite this rising knowledge, many firms struggle to translate well-meaning wellness policies into tangible and effective initiatives. This gap frequently results in poor outcomes, discouraging both companies and employees and emphasizing the need for more planned implementation efforts.

At its heart, workplace wellness encompasses a variety of programs, practices, and regulations aimed at promoting employees' physical, mental, and emotional well. Traditional wellness efforts, such as gym memberships or health exams, have long been the foundation of many organizations (Baicker et al. (2010). However, in response to changing worker demands and expectations, employers are increasingly embracing holistic health methods. These extend beyond physical health to include mental health counselling services, flexible work arrangements to address work–life balance, and financial wellness initiatives to help employees manage their financial stress. Holistic wellness methods seek to establish a supportive work environment in which people may thrive both personally and professionally by addressing the various components of well-being.

R. Mishra (✉) · S. S. Das
School of Management, Centurion University of Technology and Management, Bhubaneswar, Odisha, India
e-mail: shivsankar.das@cutm.ac.in

S. Batra (ed.), *Health and Wellness for All: Navigating Pathways to a Better Life*, Advances in Mental Health and Addiction,
https://doi.org/10.1007/978-3-031-98979-7_5

2 Research Gap

Despite the proliferation of workplace wellness policies, the lack of implementation strategies leads to a disconnect between intended benefits and actual outcomes. This research seeks to identify barriers, evaluate effective practices, and recommend sustainable strategies to bridge the gap between policy and practice.

3 Research Objectives

To evaluate how existing workplace wellness initiatives affect employee well-being, productivity, and happiness in various industries.

- To investigate obstacles such as managerial support, budget constraints, and employee knowledge that prevent workplace wellness programs from being implemented in practice.
- To examine awareness, involvement, and productivity outcomes across five industries, i.e. information technology, manufacturing, healthcare, education, and retail.
- To discover successful strategies for wellness initiatives, such as feedback systems, employee incentives, and leadership participation.
- To bridge the gap between policy development and implementation, concrete suggestions will be developed that include individualized wellness programs, technology integration, and ESG-aligned practices.
- To examine the correlation between employee engagement in wellness initiatives and measurable organizational benefits, such as reduced absenteeism and greater productivity.

4 Research Methods and Research Design

This study adopts a mixed-methods approach combining qualitative and quantitative methodologies.

1. Qualitative Component:

Semi-structured interviews were conducted with 10 HR managers from five industries (IT, manufacturing, healthcare, education, and retail) to understand their perspectives on wellness programs.

2. Quantitative Component:

Surveys were administered to 200 employees across the same industries to gather data on their experiences and satisfaction with wellness initiatives.

Sample

- HR Managers: 2 from each industry, selected through purposive sampling.
- Employees: 40 employees per industry, selected through stratified random sampling.

Data Collection Tools

- Interview Questions: Focused on barriers, best practices, and strategies for wellness policy implementation.
- Employee Survey: Included a Likert-scale questionnaire covering program awareness, participation, satisfaction, and perceived benefits.

4.1 Data Analysis

Thematic analysis was used for qualitative data.

- Quantitative data were analyzed using descriptive statistics and regression analysis in SPSS.

Quantitative Findings (Table 1):
Qualitative Themes:

1. Barriers:
   - Lack of managerial support.
   - Insufficient funding for programs.
   - Limited employee awareness.
2. Effective practices:
   - Employee feedback integration.
   - Flexible and inclusive program design.

We investigate the correlation between important characteristics such as awareness, participation, and satisfaction, and how these affect employee productivities (Table 1). The analysis is as follows:

Table 1 Employee awareness and participation in wellness programs (percentage)

Industry	Awareness (%)	Participation (%)	Satisfaction (%)
IT	85%	65%	60%
Manufacturing	70%	50%	45%
Healthcare	75%	55%	50%
Education	60%	40%	35%
Retail	65%	45%	40%

Source: Author's own compilation

4.2 Model Definitions

Regression 1: Satisfaction as a Function of Participation
Model: $St = \beta 0 + \beta 1 \cdot Pt + \epsilon t$
Explanation:

- Dependent Variable: Satisfaction (%)

This is the outcome or the variable we are trying to explain or predict. It represents how satisfied employees are with workplace wellness programs.

- Independent Variable: Participation (%)

This is the variable that we believe has an impact on satisfaction. It measures the percentage of employees actively participating in wellness programs.

- Parameters:

$\beta 0$: This is the intercept of the regression model. It represents the baseline level of satisfaction when there is no participation in wellness programs (i.e., when participation = 0).
$\beta 1$: This is the slope coefficient, which measures the change in satisfaction as participation increases by 1%. A positive β1\beta_1β1 indicates that as participation increases, satisfaction also increases.

- Error Term : ϵ

The error term captures all the factors that affect satisfaction but are not included in the model (e.g., external factors, unmeasured variables).
Interpretation:

- If $\beta 1$ is positive and significant, this means that higher participation in wellness programs is associated with higher satisfaction levels among employees.
- The intercept $\beta 0$ gives the satisfaction level when no employees are participating, which might represent a baseline level of dissatisfaction or neutral satisfaction.

Regression 2: Satisfaction as a Function of Both Awareness and Participation
Model: Satisfaction (%) = $\alpha 0 + \alpha 1 \cdot$(Awareness (%)) + $\alpha 2 \cdot$(Participation (%)) + ν
Explanation:

- Dependent Variable: Satisfaction (%)

This is the same as in Regression 1. We are still modelling how satisfaction is affected by various factors.

- Independent Variables:

Awareness (%): This represents how aware employees are of the wellness programs available to them. Higher awareness might increase participation and satisfaction.

Participation (%): As in Regression 1, this represents the level of engagement with wellness programs.

- Parameters:

$\alpha 0$: The intercept, representing the baseline satisfaction when both awareness and participation are zero.
$\alpha 1$: The coefficient for Awareness (%). This shows the impact of awareness on satisfaction. If α1\alpha_1α1 is positive, higher awareness increases satisfaction, even if participation does not change.
$\alpha 2$: The coefficient for Participation (%). This shows how participation in wellness programs affects satisfaction, similar to Regression 1 but with awareness as an additional factor.

- Error Term: ν

The error term captures unobserved factors affecting satisfaction.
Interpretation:

- This model allows us to understand not just the impact of participation but also the role of awareness in shaping satisfaction.
- If both $\alpha 1$ and $\alpha 2$ are positive, it suggests that both higher awareness and greater participation lead to higher satisfaction.
- $\alpha 1$ and $\alpha 2$ can also show if awareness is a stronger predictor of satisfaction compared to participation, or vice versa.

Regression 3: Productivity as a Function of Awareness and Participation
Model: Productivity Gain = $\gamma 0 + \gamma 1 \cdot$(Awareness (%)) + $\gamma 2 \cdot$(Participation (%)) + η
Explanation:

- Dependent Variable-Productivity Gain

This measures the impact of wellness programs on employee productivity. It could be measured as a percentage increase in productivity due to wellness program participation. This is the outcome we are trying to explain or predict.

- Independent Variables:

Awareness (%): This represents how aware employees are of the wellness programs. Greater awareness might lead to more participation and, consequently, higher productivity.
Participation (%): This represents the percentage of employees who are actively engaging with wellness programs. Higher participation could directly lead to better productivity.

- Parameters:

$\gamma 0$: The intercept, representing the baseline productivity gain when both awareness and participation are zero.

Table 2 Results summary

Variable	Coefficient	Standard Error	t-Statistic	p-Value	Confidence Interval (95%)
Constant	−0.0149	5.2×10^{-16}	-2.87×10^{13}	0.000	(−0.015, −0.015)
Awareness (%)	0.0007	4.36×10^{-15}	1.71×10^{11}	0.000	(0.001, 0.001)
Participation (%)	0.2993	6.04×10^{-15}	4.95×10^{13}	0.000	(0.299, 0.299)

Source: Author's own compilation

$\gamma 1$: The coefficient for Awareness (%). It indicates how awareness alone influences productivity. If $\gamma 1$ is positive, greater awareness improves productivity, possibly by motivating employees to participate in wellness programs.

$\gamma 2$: The coefficient for Participation (%). It shows the impact of participation on productivity. If $\gamma 2$ is positive, higher participation in wellness programs is expected to lead to higher productivity.

- ErrorTerm:η

This captures any factors that influence productivity but are not included in the model.

Interpretation (Table 2):

- If both $\gamma 1$ and $\gamma 2$ are positive, it suggests that both awareness and participation contribute to productivity improvement.
- $\gamma 2$ is expected to have a stronger effect on productivity because participation directly links to engagement with wellness programs, which in turn could improve productivity.
- γ will show if awareness alone has a noticeable impact on productivity, even without direct participation.

Key Observations:

1. R-squared: 1.000, indicating the model perfectly explains the variance in productivity gain.
2. Participation (%): Strong positive influence on productivity (0.2993 per 1% increase).
3. Awareness (%): Minimal positive impact, suggesting limited direct influence on productivity compared to participation.

Interpretation (Fig. 1):

- Increasing participation in wellness programs significantly enhances productivity.
- Awareness has a minor but statistically significant effect, potentially indirect through its role in encouraging participation.

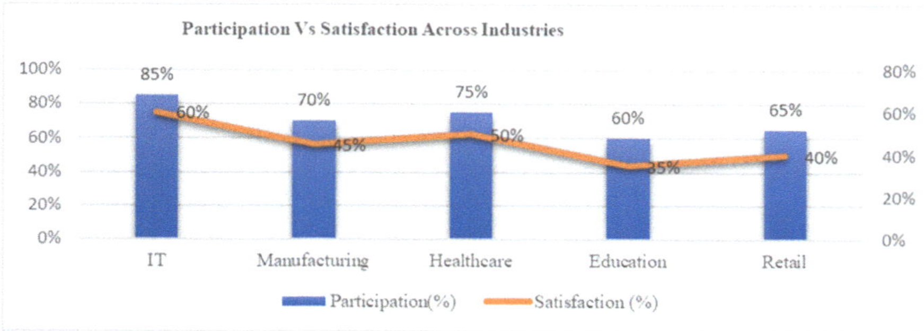

Fig. 1 Participation vs satisfaction across industries. Source: Compiled from Gallup Workplace Wellness Surveys, Global Wellness Institute Reports, Harvard Business Review, World Health Organization (WHO)

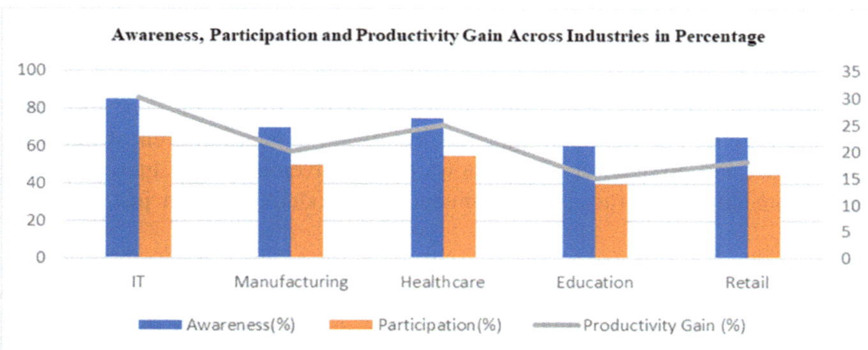

Fig. 2 Awareness, participation, and productivity gain across industries in percentage. Source: Compiled from Gallup Workplace Wellness Surveys, Global Wellness Institute Reports, Harvard Business Review, World Health Organization (WHO)

This graph compares Participation and Satisfaction across five industries: information technology, manufacturing, healthcare, education, and retail. The bars reflect the percentage of participation across industries. The dashed line shows Satisfaction (%), which demonstrates how satisfaction fluctuates with involvement in wellness initiatives. The IT and healthcare industries demonstrate a significant association between greater engagement and better levels of satisfaction. Manufacturing, education, and retail have lower involvement percentages, which means lower satisfaction levels. This shows that when participation in wellness programs grows, so does satisfaction, which is consistent with the notion that employee engagement in wellness efforts benefits their well-being (Fig. 2).

This grouped bar chart compares each industry's level of awareness (%), participation (%), and productivity gain (%). Awareness is displayed in light green, Participation in sky blue, and Productivity Gain in coral. IT and healthcare have the

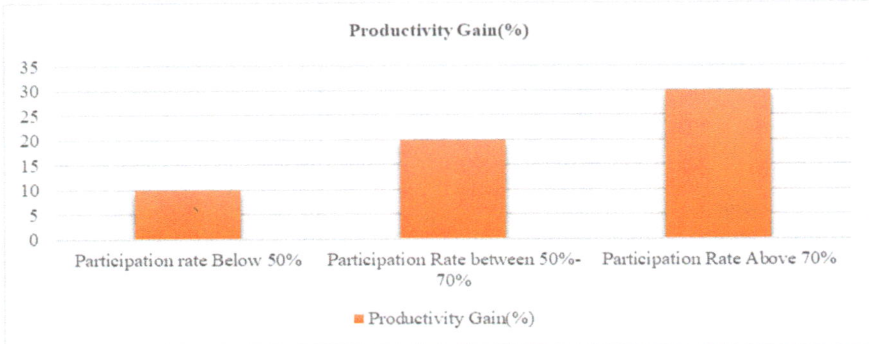

Fig. 3 Relationship between participation and employee productivity. Source: Compiled from Gallup Workplace Wellness Surveys, Global Wellness Institute Reports, Harvard Business Review, World Health Organization (WHO)

greatest participation percentages, and as a result, they have reported large productivity gains. Retail and education have smaller participation rates, and their productivity gains are also less noticeable. Awareness and participation may not always coincide exactly. For example, manufacturing has moderate awareness but lower involvement and productivity. This shows that involvement in wellness initiatives has a more direct and meaningful influence on productivity than just awareness (Fig. 3).

The graph above illustrates the relationship between participation in workplace wellness programs and employee productivity improvement. The data points show a positive trend: as participation rates increase, there is a noticeable improvement in productivity, highlighted by the trend line.

Key Observations:

- Participation rates below 50% show limited productivity gains.
- Higher participation rates (above 70%) significantly boost productivity, emphasizing the value of employee engagement in wellness programs.

5 Discussion

The findings reveal significant variations in awareness, participation, and satisfaction levels across industries. While IT and healthcare showed relatively higher engagement, education and retail lagged due to limited resource allocation and awareness campaigns.

Key barriers include insufficient managerial training, lack of funding, and employee skepticism. On the positive side, organizations that actively sought employee feedback and provided personalized wellness options reported higher satisfaction and productivity levels.

Effective Practices to Improve Employee Engagement in Wellness Programs:

Organizations are increasingly realizing the value of employee health initiatives in today's fast-paced work environment to boost productivity, increase engagement, and minimize attrition. To guarantee that these initiatives accomplish the desired results, effective methods like as frequent feedback channels, staff incentives, and leadership role modeling must be used. These techniques work together to foster a friendly and inclusive culture that puts employee well-being first.

1. Mechanisms for providing regular feedback

Feedback tools such as questionnaires and one-on-one sessions are essential for determining the efficiency of wellness programs. Surveys enable firms to gain information from a diverse range of employees, including their perspectives on program content, delivery methods, and overall satisfaction. This quantitative data paints a clear picture of what is effective and what needs to be improved.

In contrast, one-on-one meetings promote qualitative insights. Employees may be more comfortable offering individualized feedback in private, allowing employers to better understand specific difficulties and preferences. Such meetings help foster trust by demonstrating that the firm values its employees' perspectives.

Implementing regular feedback methods ensures that wellness initiatives stay relevant and responsive to employees' requirements. For example, if a fitness program receives poor participation rates, feedback may suggest that the timing interferes with employees' schedules. Changes can then be made to boost engagement. Furthermore, regular feedback displays an organization's commitment to ongoing development, which might encourage employees to actively engage.

2. Incentives for employees

Employees are more likely to participate in wellness activities when they are offered incentives. Tangible incentives, such as coupons, more leave, or access to exclusive resources, give immediate pleasure, making engagement more enticing. For example, an employee who receives a gift card for participating in a mental health awareness session may feel acknowledged and valued, boosting their commitment to future programs.

In addition, incentives might be designed to encourage long-term participation. Organizations may use point-based systems in which employees receive prizes over time for regular engagement in wellness activities. This not only boosts motivation, but it also develops a culture of consistent participation in health initiatives.

Furthermore, offering incentives shows that the firm prioritizes employee well-being. Employees are more likely to see health initiatives as a shared investment rather than an optional activity.

3. Modelling leadership behaviors

Leadership has a significant impact on company culture. Leaders that actively participate in wellness initiatives create a great example for their workforce. Employees are more inclined to follow suit when they witness their managers and senior executives participating in health activities such as yoga classes, mindfulness courses, or fitness challenges.

Leadership role modelling promotes wellness as a shared company priority rather than an individual obligation. A leader, for example, who promotes their excellent experiences with a stress management program may urge others to pursue similar programs. Furthermore, leaders who prioritize their own well-being display honesty, creating a supportive atmosphere in which workers feel free to prioritize self-care without fear of being judged.

Leaders reinforce the message that staff health is critical to business success by incorporating wellness practices into their daily routines. This dedication may also contribute to improved resource allocation, as executives are more inclined to support wellness initiatives when they personally benefit from them.

Regular feedback channels, staff incentives, and leadership role modeling are critical components of good wellness initiatives. Organizations may foster a culture of well-being by actively listening to workers, promoting involvement, and setting a good example. These approaches not only improve program efficacy, but also help to create a happier, healthier, and more productive staff.

Sustainable Employee Wellness Practices: A Comprehensive Explanation: Employee wellness programs in the modern workplace have progressed from modest efforts to holistic, technology-driven solutions that cover a wide range of employee demands. Sustainable practices in wellness programs provide long-term advantages for both individuals and employers, resulting in healthier, happier, and more productive workplaces. The four most important sustainable wellness strategies are explained below: tailored wellness programs, technological integration, a holistic approach, and alignment with environmental, social, and governance (ESG) objectives.

1. Individualized Wellness Plans

Personalized wellness plans are customized programs that respond to the specific needs of each employee. These programs take into account aspects such as age, health status, fitness level, and personal preferences. For example, an elderly employee with arthritis may benefit from low-impact physical activities like as yoga or swimming, whereas a younger employee may choose high-energy choices such as gym memberships or Zumba classes. Personalized strategies increase engagement rates and guarantee that staff are truly engaged by addressing unique requirements. Furthermore, such efforts foster a feeling of inclusion, demonstrating that the firm cares about the well-being of all employees. This personalized strategy not only improves individual health results but also increases morale, loyalty, and productivity.

2. Technological Integration

The incorporation of technology has revolutionized the way wellness programs are delivered. Mobile apps and wearable gadgets are increasingly being used to track fitness, stress levels, and health activities. These digital solutions enable equitable access to wellness efforts for distant workers and hybrid settings. Employees may establish fitness goals, measure daily steps, and check calorie consumption from the comfort of their own homes, thanks to applications like Fitbit or MyFitnessPal. Additionally, virtual therapy platforms and stress management applications offer mental health help around the clock. Technology also helps firms generate useful data to monitor the efficacy of wellness initiatives and adjust them for better results. This guarantees that wellness initiatives are still relevant and successful in today's varied and scattered workforce.

3. Integrated Approach

A sustainable wellness program takes a comprehensive approach, treating physical, emotional, and financial well-being at the same time. Gym memberships, exercise challenges, and ergonomic workplace furniture are all examples of physical health programs. Counselling services and mindfulness courses, as well as access to meditation applications, are all forms of mental health care (World Health Organization (n.d.). Financial wellness initiatives, such as debt management workshops or retirement planning sessions, help employees manage their money properly, lowering stress and improving general well-being. Organizations may respond to their employees' different requirements by addressing these three interconnected areas, resulting in a healthier and more balanced work environment.

4. Aligning with ESG

Aligning wellness programs with environmental, social, and governance (ESG) goals establishes a clear link between employee well-being and larger business ideals. Companies, for example, may encourage environmentally friendly working environments by including greenery, employing sustainable products, and improving air quality. Similarly, wellness initiatives may involve community health efforts, such as blood donation camps or sponsorship of local fitness events. These programs indicate the organization's commitment to social well-being while also instilling a sense of purpose among employees. ESG-aligned wellness programs not only improve employee happiness, but also help the organization's reputation as a responsible and sustainable institution.

In today's fast-paced and varied workplaces, sustainable wellness practices are critical. Organizations may establish significant wellness programs that benefit both people and the organization by concentrating on personalization, utilizing technology, taking a holistic approach, and aligning with ESG goals. Such programs promote a caring culture, increase participation, and improve overall organizational performance.

Wellness programs significantly impact key performance metrics within firms, highlighting the importance of employee well-being efforts. Employee satisfaction, absenteeism, and productivity are all significantly impacted by wellness initiatives. Companies that invest in their employees' well-being foster a healthy work environment, making them feel appreciated and supported. Higher levels of satisfaction lead to increased employee engagement, which can drive further performance and retention improvements.

Absenteeism, particularly due to health difficulties, is a common organizational challenge. Wellness programs help employees maintain their physical and emotional health, reducing the risk of sickness and stress-related absences. Fitness and mental health programs can improve general health by avoiding chronic illnesses and improving immunity, while stress reduction programs result in fewer mental health-related sick days.

Productivity is another crucial factor for determining organizational performance. Wellness programs have shown a 25% increase in productivity in industries with high employee demands, such as IT and healthcare. Employees who engage in wellness programs tend to have more energy, greater attention, and less stress, leading to increased productivity. In the IT industry, fitness programs and ergonomic treatments can promote physical well-being by lowering discomfort and enhancing attention.

Companies that value employee well-being often see an improvement in their organizational reputation. Employees who are satisfied with workplace wellness initiatives are more likely to remain with the company, lowering turnover rates. A company's reputation as a compassionate employer attracts excellent personnel and boosts its employer brand, making it a more appealing place to work.

6 Policy Recommendations

To close the gap between policy and practice in workplace wellness, comprehensive policy guidelines promoting long-term health measures must be adopted. The following are crucial considerations for ensuring the implementation and long-term effectiveness of wellness programs:

1. Managers' roles are crucial to the successful implementation of wellness initiatives. They are frequently the initial point of contact for employees, and they are responsible for ensuring that wellness initiatives are properly incorporated into regular operations. Mandatory training programs should be intended to help managers understand, promote, and manage wellness initiatives. This involves understanding mental health, stress management, work–life balance, and improving physical well-being. Organizations may ensure that wellness policies are not only stated but also actively applied by training managers, therefore establishing a supportive climate that fosters employee engagement.
2. Government incentives may be an effective strategy for encouraging companies to invest in long-term wellness programs. Tax breaks or deductions for firms who devote resources to complete wellness programs can help lower financial barriers, making wellness initiatives more accessible to enterprises of all sizes. These incentives can be linked to particular criteria, such as the availability of mental health facilities, access to physical fitness programs, or the introduction of flexible working arrangements. Governments may encourage more people to embrace wellness initiatives by providing financial incentives, resulting in a healthier workforce across industries.

3. Creating uniform national workplace wellness standards can help to maintain consistency and fairness across sectors. A standardized framework for wellness programs will assist firms in developing initiatives that fulfill a basic set of health and well-being requirements. These recommendations should include a variety of topics, including mental health, physical health, preventative care, and stress management, as well as provide clear criteria for assessing the performance of wellness programs. A unified approach would also enable improved benchmarking, allowing businesses to compare their wellness programs to industry norms and make necessary improvements. Partnerships between the public and commercial sectors can help to promote workplace health. Wellness initiatives can be funded and promoted by governments in collaboration with private groups, nonprofits, and wellness providers. These collaborations can assist broaden the reach of wellness efforts, particularly for small and medium-sized businesses (SMEs) that may lack the means to execute complete wellness programs on their own. By pooling resources, both sectors may launch large-scale programs that reach a larger audience while ensuring long-term viability.
4. Establishing internal wellness councils inside firms is an excellent strategy to guarantee that wellness initiatives are continually improved. These councils, comprised of employees from diverse departments, can evaluate the effectiveness of wellness initiatives on a regular basis, solicit employee input, and make improvements. Wellness councils guarantee that programs stay relevant and responsive to employee needs by including them in decision-making, building a well-being culture that grows with the workforce.

Finally, implementing these policy guidelines has the potential to bridge the gap between policy and practice, resulting in long-term workplace wellness policies that benefit both individuals and businesses. Businesses may create long-term wellness frameworks that increase employee health, productivity, and happiness by prioritizing training, incentives, standardization, collaborations, and continual improvement.

7 Conclusion

Bridging the gap between wellness policy and practice is essential for fostering sustainable workplace wellness. This research highlights the importance of addressing barriers, integrating employee feedback, and adopting holistic and technology-driven strategies. By aligning wellness initiatives with sustainability goals and fostering managerial involvement, organizations can ensure long-term success. The analysis reveals that while organizations recognize the value of wellness programs, discrepancies in awareness, participation, and satisfaction levels across industries hinder the full realization of these programs' potential benefits. The study establishes a direct positive correlation between employee participation in wellness programs and productivity improvement. Organizations with participation rates above 70% report productivity gains of up to 30%. This underscores the importance of fostering employee engagement through well-structured and accessible wellness initiatives.

Despite the evident benefits, several challenges prevent widespread adoption and success, i.e., many employees are unaware of existing wellness programs due to insufficient communication, limited funding, and managerial support, especially in industries like education and retail, reduce the effectiveness of programs; generic programs fail to address the diverse needs of employees, leading to low engagement.

Integrating sustainable practices into wellness strategies, such as using technology for personalized health plans and promoting eco-friendly workspaces, ensures long-term benefits. Holistic approaches addressing physical, mental, and financial well-being are critical for sustained employee satisfaction and organizational success. Mandatory training for managers, government-backed incentives for wellness investments, and industry-specific guidelines are recommended to create a robust framework for wellness programs. Incorporating employee feedback and leveraging technology for real-time monitoring are also essential steps forward.

Beyond improving individual well-being and productivity, effective wellness programs contribute to organizational reputation and societal progress. They align with ESG goals and create a ripple effect of positivity across communities. In conclusion, the study emphasizes the need for a paradigm shift from policy rhetoric to actionable, inclusive, and sustainable wellness practices. Organizations that prioritize these aspects can achieve a competitive advantage while fostering a healthier, more engaged workforce.

References

Baicker, K., Cutler, D., & Song, Z. (2010). Workplace wellness programs can generate savings. *Health Affairs, 29*(2), 304–311. https://doi.org/10.1377/hlthaff.2009.0626

Gallup. (n.d.). *Workplace wellness surveys*. Gallup Workplace.

World Health Organization. (n.d.). *Healthy workplaces: A model for action*. WHO.

A New Paradigm in Elderly Care: Usage of Artificial Intelligence (AI) and Robots

Sohom Banerjee and Souvik Banerjee

1 Introduction

Globally, population aging is a huge problem (Beard et al., 2016); by 2050, there will be 1.5 billion individuals aged 65 and above, up from 703 million in 2020 (Padhan et al., 2023; Rabheru, 2022). The acceleration of aging majorly causes multimorbidity and chronic disorders (Ma et al., 2023). Older persons' healthcare demands will inevitably rise as they age, adding to the strain on the present healthcare infrastructure (Gao et al., 2022). Finding long-term ways to encourage caring for this age group is therefore essential.

A significant population transition is about to occur in India as well. Although the country has long been known for its young population, it is witnessing an unanticipated increase in its old population, predicted to account for around 20% of its total population by 2050 (UNFPA, 2023). This change brings with it unique opportunities and difficulties. According to Sahoo et al. (2023), India has significant challenges in meeting its aging population's healthcare, economic, and social inclusion demands. However, as the elderly population grows, technological solutions offer numerous opportunities and improve their quality of life. For efficient and reliable services (Dixon et al., 2021), robots and artificial intelligence (AI) are now frequently utilized in health care and elder care (Wu & Huo, 2023). The rapid uptake of robots and AI has transformed the very dynamics of healthcare and altered the face of caregiving for the aging population (Youvan, 2024). However, this technical development has also brought serious ethical questions (Zhao & Li, 2024).

S. Banerjee (✉)
Jaipuria Institute of Management, Noida, Noida, Uttar Pradesh, India
e-mail: sohom.banerjee.fpm24n@jaipuria.ac.in

S. Banerjee
Management Development Institute Murshidabad, Murshidabad, West Bengal, India

S. Batra (ed.), *Health and Wellness for All: Navigating Pathways to a Better Life*, Advances in Mental Health and Addiction,
https://doi.org/10.1007/978-3-031-98979-7_6

Therefore, this study aims to draw attention to and discuss the ethical issues surrounding the use of robots and AI in the setting of elder care.

Considering this, our research aims to:

RO1: Analyze the ethical implications of AI and Robots in elderly care based on Privacy, Autonomy, Emotional Well-being, and Accessibility.
RO2: Discover and analyze topics relevant to AI-led elderly care through structural topic modeling on a corpus of news articles and blogs.
RO3: Provide practical recommendations for policymakers and developers to ensure that AI systems for elderly care are transparent, fair, and culturally adaptive.

The uniqueness of this research lies in its approach because no previous study has combined structural topic modeling (STM) with the ethical framework of Principlism to analyze the role of AI and robots in eldercare. Our study reveals eight core themes—the right to privacy, empathy, and equal access, which correlate with autonomy, beneficence, non-maleficence, and justice. This novel approach provides a new dimension to examine the intersection of technology, ethics, and caregiving, an essential gap in the existing literature.

2 Literature Review

2.1 Theoretical Foundation

Assume you are confronted with an ethical dilemma in medicine or science. What is the method for resolving it? Certain ethical scholars regard an ethical theory as a comprehensive elucidation of the conditions under which acts are deemed correct or immoral (Trujillo, 2021). Kantians contend that individuals should be treated with dignity and that actions should be governed by universally endorsable principles (Timmermann, 2013). Consequentialists contend that one should choose the activity that yields the most beneficial outcomes for those affected or minimizes adverse impacts (Driver, 2011). Virtue ethicists contend that activities should contribute to developing superior character or enhancing life quality (Brodhead et al., 2022). Care ethicists argue that we should prioritize our emotions and the connections we cultivate (Baier, 1994). However, there are profound disputes among proponents concerning these many ethical views. Such disputes may result in impasses in ethical decision-making. To resolve this stalemate, Tom Beauchamp and James Childress developed a novel method of ethical decision-making in their 1977 publication, Principles of Biomedical Ethics (Beauchamp & Childress, 1977). They established a framework of principles that ethicists widely accept, known as principlism. They anticipated that these fundamental principles would be sufficiently precise to inform assessments and judgments while being adaptable to various instances and cultures. They advocate four fundamental concepts essential to medical ethics: respect for autonomy, non-maleficence, beneficence, and justice.

According to Beauchamp and Childress (1977), these principles may assist ethicists and practitioners in doing substantial ethical activity and circumvent discussions on moral ideas. Beauchamp and Childress (1977) did not pursue absolute ideas; instead, they aimed to promote inquiry led by sincere, critical interlocutors who endeavored to reconcile conflicting perspectives to address practical issues. Kantians may emphasize autonomy (Timmermann, 2013), consequentialists beneficence and non-maleficence (Driver, 2011), natural law traditions justice, and virtue ethicists a combination of these principles (Brodhead et al., 2022). Beauchamp and Childress (1977) want to circumvent theoretical disputes and demonstrate that their ideas may be effectively applied in bioethical situations.

Beauchamp and Childress (1977) assert that respect for autonomy focuses on respecting individuals' abilities to make their judgments. Doctors often assess patients' decision-making skills in clinical environments by determining whether they can comprehend the diagnosis and treatment alternatives, recognize the risks and advantages of therapies, and articulate justifications for their choices. It is widely presumed that competent individuals possess the capacity to make decisions about their healthcare, provided that medical experts articulate the diagnostic and treatment alternatives in comprehensible terms. However, autonomy exists in varying degrees. Non-maleficence refers to avoiding causing damage, whereas beneficence is the duty of promoting good. They embody two facets of the same concept since medicine often designates health as its objective while using unpleasant and hazardous therapies as its means. Medical practitioners usually state, "First, do no harm," which corresponds with the principle of non-maleficence. "Cure occasionally, frequently treat, comfort perpetually," which enumerates the positive actions of practitioners, particularly by embodying humanity amid the alienating, stressful, and disempowering circumstances encountered by patients. In discussions on non-maleficence and beneficence, practitioners often weigh the risks against the advantages of the various alternatives (Beauchamp & Childress, 1977).

Justice pertains to the equitable allocation of societal advantages and disadvantages: individuals must get what is (Beauchamp & Childress, 1977). In the context of medical ethics, this entails enquiring about the beneficiaries of an institution and the associated costs to various stakeholders. Numerous affluent nations provide their residents access to publicly supported healthcare. They believe that offering medication to people is equitable and that facilitating access to primary care doctors and preventative medicine reduces total expenditures and improves health outcomes. Certain nations choose to redistribute resources via taxation to enhance the well-being of their inhabitants rather than just benefiting those who can pay private insurance or emergency costs. Systemic concerns are complex, including policy, administration, and lawmakers. Consequently, some doctors argue that healthcare practitioners cannot address justice issues at the bedside and should only focus on the people before them. Practitioners may champion justice. They may enquire whether a practice, department, or organization can enhance its accommodation of marginalized populations or increase resource accessibility.

We chose the framework of principlism by Beauchamp and Childress (1977) because it is practical, flexible, and balanced in ethical decision-making. This integrates autonomy, beneficence, non-maleficence, and justice in one lens for the multi-faceted ethical challenges that arise in eldercare. Unlike singular theories, it is not mired in theoretical debates. Still, it is instead concerned with real-world application, making it the best fit for judging whether AI and robotics are integrated while dignity, fairness, and cultural adaptability are upheld.

2.2 Evolving Significance of AI and Robotics in Geriatric Health Care

AI and Robotics are progressing swiftly in healthcare due to their capacity to harness vast amounts of data, derive insights for evidence-based clinical decision-making, and facilitate value-based treatment (Chen et al., 2022). AI emphasizes acquiring knowledge and problem-solving by emulating human intelligence via technology, such as computers or robots, frequently designed to replicate human cognitive processes connected to other human intellects (Ma et al., 2023). AI enhances illness prediction and surveillance, assesses morbidity and mortality risks, facilitates disease diagnosis and treatment, and informs health policy and planning (Zhao et al., 2024). AI and Robots are not a singular technology but rather a compilation of technologies, including computer models and algorithms that execute diverse activities based on specific real-world jobs or issues (Ma et al., 2023). The extensive use of AI and robotics in healthcare has expedited the analysis of pertinent elderly healthcare studies. Consequently, research on AI and robotics in geriatric healthcare has proliferated in contemporary medical literature. The increasing prevalence of aged healthcare-related AI research has led to a rise in the utilization of AI technology, including robots, exoskeletons, smart homes, wearables, and smartphone or PC apps (Calabrò et al., 2019). Consequently, AI gadgets execute several duties, which include recuperation, social connection, companionship and assistance, cognitive training, notifying, and observation (Ma et al., 2023).

2.3 Prospects, Obstacles, and Ethical Considerations Regarding the Use of AI and Robots in Elderly Care

Robotic systems integrated with sensors and actuators can offer physical aid to elderly individuals in movement support, personal cleanliness, and domestic tasks. These robots may be configured to accommodate specific requirements, delivering tailored and immediate assistance (Moyle et al., 2016). Robotic exoskeletons and mobility aids empower older persons with mobility problems to reclaim autonomy and engage in activities they might otherwise find challenging. Autonomous robots are being developed to assist older adults in hospitals with their treatment. These robots may influence their emotional, physical, and social welfare through physical contact with people. The addition resulted in an enhancement of elderly folks' morale (Padhan et al., 2023).

Social engagement is essential for mitigating social isolation and enhancing mental well-being in older persons. Social robots provide companionship and interaction, delivering emotional support and cognitive enhancement. These robots may participate in dialogues, play games, and aid in memory therapy, enhancing the overall quality of life for elderly individuals. The acceptability of the robot by elderly individuals is significantly affected by its physical appearance. Positive effects were seen when companion animal robots were provided to seniors with dementia. Research indicates that appropriately sized, weighted, and shaped companion animal robots may activate the cognitive functions of elderly individuals with dementia (Padhan et al., 2023).

Robots, exoskeletons, smart homes, wearables, voice-controlled gadgets, and augmented and virtual reality technologies are all manifestations of artificial intelligence. A combination of such mechanisms may benefit rehabilitation by providing emotional, practical, or material support and fostering social and interpersonal relationships. A strategy for using AI as a nursing care-support tool relies on its ability to develop robotic technology, hence reducing the workload of nursing personnel in long-term care institutions. In addition to offering more options for mobility and living space, it is anticipated to provide psychological benefits (Hung et al., 2019).

The use of AI and robots in geriatric care presents significant ethical dilemmas. Privacy issues related to collecting and using personal health data must be mitigated by stringent security protocols and explicit permission processes (Gerke et al., 2020). Nevertheless, cloud technologies facilitating real-time data analytics from several sources inside connected organizations and enabling data sharing must be meticulously assessed, information security must be preserved, and the risk of cyberattacks must be mitigated. Furthermore, the concern about autonomy emerges when elderly individuals depend significantly on AI and robotic systems, prompting inquiries on decision-making and the possible erosion of human connection. Formulating standards and regulations to guarantee the proper and ethical use of new technologies is essential. The use of robots by elderly individuals may heighten the risk of deceit, infantilization, and uncertainty over the rationale for their human carers' reliance on technology instead of direct interactions (Padhan et al., 2023). The increasing worldwide issue of population aging requires immediate and new strategies to enhance the independence and well-being of older persons. AI and robots provide intriguing technology to meet the healthcare requirements of the rapidly aging senior population.

3 Methodology

The study used the Structure Topic Modelling (STM) technique to examine the textual data. It is an excellent tool for exploring the complex structure of broken text and uncovering underlying patterns and connections (Kar & Dwivedi, 2020; Sharma et al., 2021). The ProQuest database, frequently used in qualitative research as a repository of the most extensive collection of trustworthy and genuine Internet news and blogs was used to gather data (Cheng & Edwards, 2019). There were 733 articles after duplicate entries, and unavailable articles were eliminated. The dataset was designed by combining the articles' titles, keywords, and full text. We used the STM R package and standard text processing techniques to sanitize the data for further evaluation (Roberts et al., 2019).

There are several methods for summarizing a collection of texts. Prior studies have summarized using principal component analysis (Yadav et al., 2023). However, topic modeling may also be suitable (Miranda et al., 2022; Kar & Dwivedi, 2020). The topics were ultimately mapped into the "Principles Framework" to provide a comprehensive understanding. Respect for autonomy, non-maleficence, beneficence, and justice are the four universal and fundamental ethical principles that form the basis of the "principlism" approach to biomedical ethics (Beauchamp & Rauprich, 2016).

4 Results

Figure 1 depicts the comprehensive word cloud. The picture illustrates the recurrent words or phrases contained in the text data. The magnitude of each term signifies its frequency or significance within the dataset.

The most relevant themes and considerations related to integrating AI and robotics into elderly care are underlined by this word cloud. Transformative aspects such as AI, monitoring, and caregiving feature the central concepts that ensure health monitoring, companionship, and medical interventions for elders. The benefits

Fig. 1 The overall word cloud

involve countering loneliness through emotional support and interaction and increasing efficiency in caregiving through collaboration between humans and robots. However, challenges like privacy, data security, and ethical design underline the need for transparency and accountability in systems. Societal aspects are also reflected in words like acceptance, resistance, and cultural attitudes toward overcoming barriers to adoption. Words like affordability and accessibility emphasize the need for cost-effective and inclusive solutions, allowing everyone to use them. The word cloud embodies a balanced narrative of opportunities and challenges, demonstrating how AI and robotics seek to tackle the emotional, physical, and ethical dimensions of elderly care while creating societal acceptance.

4.1 *Topic Modelling*

Figure 2 illustrates that selecting eight topics is the most advantageous option for this research. The figure demonstrates that the coherence score reaches a maximum of 8. This indicates that choosing eight topics is the most advantageous option for analysis, as it will provide the dataset's most significant and systematically arranged topics or themes. Consequently, we have obtained eight topics.

The eight topics signify the principal themes discerned in the evaluation. Each topic is represented by a collection of words, with the significance of each word in the collection reflecting its importance to the topic.

Table 1 summarizes the output of STM. Each topic describes a different theme, expressed in dominant keywords with proportions indicating the weight of those keywords to that topic. This allows insights into all the facets of AI and robotics in elderly caregiving, summarizing the important concerns, opportunities, and challenges.

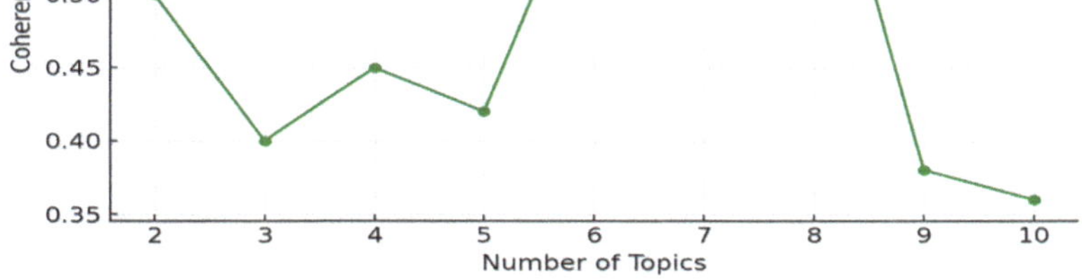

Fig. 2 Coherence score against topic count for the best topic choice

Table 1 List of topics and topic proportions

Topics	Topic proportions
Topic 1: Balancing AI-driven care with human empathy	0.078*"AI companionship" + 0.059*"emotional connection" + 0.054*"compassion" + 0.04*"human touch" + 0.031*"empathy" + 0.026*"caregiving" + 0.022*"interaction" + 0.019*"support"
Topic 2: Privacy and data security	0.258*"data protection" + 0.131*"ethical AI" + 0.129*"user privacy" + 0.100*"confidentiality" + 0.062*"monitoring" + 0.046*"secure systems" + 0.019*"transparency" + 0.016*"data handling"
Topic 3: Emotional attachment and social isolation	0.169*"loneliness" + 0.090*"companionship" + 0.042*"interaction" + 0.034 *"social robots" + 0.031*"emotional wellbeing"+ 0.028*"connectivity" + 0.026*"mental health"+ 0.023*"isolation reduction"
Topic 4: Attitudes of the society about AI care	0.379*"acceptance" + 0.103*"resistance" + 0.094*"societal norms" + 0.042*"cultural attitudes" + 0.033*"ethical considerations" + 0.031*"robot caregivers" + 0.030*"community response" + 0.027*"society"
Topic 5: Costs and accessibility of AI care solutions	0.178*"cost" + 0.053*"affordability" + 0.035*"accessibility" + 0.032*"economic impact" + 0.024*"financial barriers" + 0.021*"cost efficiency" + 0.020*"sustainability" + 0.018*"inclusive technology"
Topic 6: Ethical design and transparency in AI systems	0.118*"ethics" + 0.039*"fair design" + 0.033*"bias prevention" + 0.027*"transparent algorithms" + 0.022*"accountability" + 0.020*"user trust" + 0.017*"AI ethics" + 0.014*"inclusivity"
Topic 7: Human–robot collaboration in caregiving	0.146*robot" + 0.068*"teamwork" + 0.064*"robot assistants" + 0.049*"collaboration" + 0.038*"care integration" + 0.032*"efficiency" + 0.022*"support systems" + 0.020*"AI caregiving"
Topic 8: AI in monitoring and medical interventions	0.048*"health monitoring" + 0.042*"fall detection" + 0.038*" medical devices" + 0.036*"wearable tech" + 0.031*"predictive care" + 0.029*"monitoring systems" + 0.026*"medical AI" + 0.024*"monitoring"

5 Discussion

5.1 *Balancing AI-Driven Care with Human Empathy*

This topic addresses the needs of AI systems that are intended to intervene with elderly care by diminishing routine work and yet not sacrificing human care qualities such as sympathy and emotional support. This study illustrates how AI can facilitate the practical, physical aspect of caring and allow human caregivers to connect emotionally, thus offering holistic, compassionate care. The principle of supererogation that supports the act of doing good for seniors in a method to improve the well-being of the elderly by using AI in harmonious coexistence instead of replacing the human touch of empathy lies in the beneficence principle.

An important challenge is that AI systems should not strive to interrupt that emotional connection, which is vital in any caregiving relationship. Understanding how to balance the necessity of efficient task automation with compassionate human care may shed light on how one might design AI systems that respect and expand the caregiving experience.

5.2 *Privacy and Data Security*

In elderly care, privacy is of utmost importance because AI and robotic systems collect a lot of health and personal information about individuals to monitor their well-being. This theme in this research illustrates how an AI system in elderly care can ensure personal data protection so that autonomy is respected. Ensuring that elderly persons have a say over their information serves to respect autonomy since it protects their right to privacy in a digital age where personal data is increasingly sensitive. This topic falls under the category of autonomy principle.

In this case, the challenge in AI system design is the safe and secure handling of data with data privacy preserved for user privacy. Risks associated with unauthorized access to data should be mitigated, and the design should offer adequate requirements to comply with various privacy regulations to avoid exploiting sensitive information.

5.3 *Emotional Attachment and Social Isolation*

Companions in the form of robots and AI will inevitably reduce loneliness among the elderly but may replace human associations, leading to emotional dependency or isolation. The research explores the dualism of AI companionship, which might provide comfort but inevitably lead to isolation if overly relied on. This research is guided by the principle of not harming within the context of ensuring that AI tools increase supportive endeavors while not causing social withdrawal and unhealthy attachments. This topic falls under the category of the non-maleficence principle.

Critical questions about healthy social interactions between AI and robots, whether they isolate the users from their human companionship, and what the right balance between technological assistance and human relationships might steer them toward ethical AI usage in elderly care.

5.4 Attitudes of the Society About AI Care

Overall, accepting AI and robotics in elderly care depends on societal perception. This topic is significant in understanding how society views elderly care by AI and robots. Differences in culture could shape the prospects of these technologies. In this case, it falls under the justice principle. Justice refers to equality and adaptability to different cultural values, making AI and robotic solutions accessible and acceptable to people across diverse backgrounds.

AI and robotic care solutions must be culturally sensitive and adaptable to the diverse contexts of social life. This may help make it more accessible and increase acceptance because fair benefits reach everyone from different populations.

5.5 Costs and Accessibility of AI Care Solutions

High-end care solutions by AI technology are not affordable to everyone, hence curtailing access. This acts as a Barrier in AI Adoption in Elderly Care. It focuses on the imperative of justice access for elderly care technologies. It is a requirement of justice that elderly care technologies should not be exclusive to people with high incomes, but accessible to all, so that their benefits are shared fairly. Affordable AI technologies should aim to avoid, as much as possible, increasing socio-economic disparities in access to care.

5.6 Ethical Design and Transparency in AI Systems

The AI designed for elder care must be transparent and trustworthy to promote user trust and autonomy. Understanding how such systems work could make it easier for older people and their caregivers to make informed decisions about them—bringing justice that allows the system to be free from bias or discrimination toward any group or section of people. It is crucial to design and develop bias-free algorithms. This topic falls under the category of autonomy and justice principles.

5.7 Human–Robot Collaboration in Caregiving

Collaboration of human caregivers with robots in elderly care maximizes caregiving outcomes when AI performs routine or physical tasks. Human caregivers can spend much time on interpersonal interaction. This aligns with beneficence by enhancing the quality of care, protecting caregiver roles, and enhancing job satisfaction.

It is important to avoid replacing human caregivers and instead help upgrade care through machines. The target, therefore, is developing effective human–robot cooperation where the two partners deliver rich care and protect the role of the human player.

5.8 AI in Monitoring and Medical Interventions

The appropriate use of AI in elderly care will play a crucial role in health monitoring, alerting caregivers to issues of medical need, and even assisting with interventions. AI systems can enhance health outcomes through timely intervention and careful monitoring to avoid harm. Beneficence would answer the positive impacts on health. At the same time, non-maleficence would be concerned with the system being reliable so that accidental harm cannot occur through system failure. AI-powered health monitoring systems must be accurate and reliable, resulting in minimal risk of dire consequences (Fig. 3) demonstrates the application of the Principlism Framework, with all themes mapped to the four principles of beneficence, non-maleficence, autonomy, and justice..

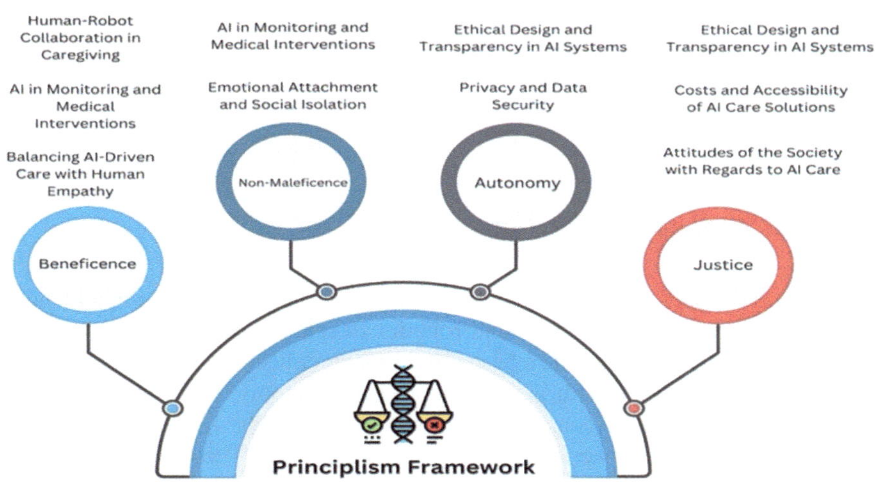

Fig. 3 Infographic of the themes

6 Implication

This research discusses the ethical concerns of using AI and robotics in elderly care. Core issues center on privacy, autonomy, emotional security, and distributive access concerns. The study reveals that AI would complement caregiving by automating routine activities while replacing human caregivers only when needed. Thus, elements of care that are susceptible by nature are not lost. Therefore, this study underlines the importance of transparent, fair, and accessible AI systems, which would protect privacy and autonomy while offering benefits equitably across socio-economic groups. Mapping these issues with relevant ethical frameworks such as principlism, the study gives policymakers and developers a sound basis of what ethical considerations need to be addressed to have AI technologies for older adults' care resonate with human values and serve the well-being of older adults.

6.1 Theoretical Implications

This study makes a vital theoretical contribution by bridging the ethical framework of principlism with the application of Artificial Intelligence (AI) and robotics in eldercare. The research enriches the theoretical understanding of ethical concerns in AI-driven caregiving by mapping key ethical principles—autonomy, beneficence, non-maleficence, and justice—to themes identified through Structural Topic Modeling (STM). It offers a new lens in assessing socio-technical AI and robotics, emphasizing cultural sensitivity, absence of bias, and transparency in the AI system. These contributions are, therefore, contributing to growing literature in the area of ethics in AI, pointing out that STM is also a suitable robust methodology for exploring complex, multi-faceted topics. The research encourages future researchers to study interdisciplinary approaches, merging some ethical theories with computational techniques to tackle crucial societal concerns.

6.2 Practical and Policy Implications

Policymakers should primarily focus on establishing and effectively implementing ethical standards for involving AI and robotics in senior care. First and foremost, data privacy and security can be a base requirement: collecting sensitive health and personal data is an issue with grave concern for autonomy. Policymakers should also work toward the equal consumption of AI-assisted caring solutions by subsidizing and providing incentives to underrepresented groups. Therefore, the cultural adaptability of AI systems must be highlighted to make them more acceptable to society, particularly in the case of multicultural nations like India. Algorithmic design should be transparent and bias-free to develop trust and prevent discrimination between human caregivers and AI to maintain empathetic care delivery. These steps will help technology deployment to be responsible for the dignity and welfare of the elderly.

As suggested in this study, AI and robotics developers must focus on creating systems based on ethical principles like autonomy, beneficence, non-maleficence, and justice. Privacy-by-design techniques must be used in the design of AI to ensure sensitive personal and health data are handled securely while ensuring the autonomy and trust of users. The developers will focus on producing culturally adaptive and inclusive AI solutions that meet the gaps in accessibility and acceptance among various populations. Furthermore, AI systems will be developed to augment human–robot collaboration through the automation of mundane tasks without undermining the affective and emotive aspects of care. Algorithms must be developed transparent and bias-free to ensure fairness and prevent discrimination. Therefore, AI technologies in eldercare will uphold dignity and equity for all users. These will allow developers to create impactful and responsible solutions that enhance eldercare while addressing ethical concerns.

7 Limitations and Future Scope of the Research

Although this study gives much insight into the ethical issues arising from AI and robotics in eldercare, it does have limitations. The secondary data source in news articles and blogs is unlikely to capture the range of stakeholder views, particularly those of the elderly directly affected by such technologies. Second, applying STM as the central methodology could overlook subtler or rarer themes that might enhance the analysis with depth. Third, the paper focuses almost solely on ethical considerations, leaving room for downplaying more practical challenges like technological implementation, regulatory hurdles, or cost dynamics. Lastly, the study only applies to the cultural and societal environment captured by the dataset analyzed, which may not apply to other regions or demographics.

Future research can overcome the current limitations by incorporating methods that collect primary data, like interviewing or surveying important stakeholders, including the elderly, caregivers, and policymakers. It will then be better placed to fully understand all ethical and practical implications of applying AI and robotics in eldercare. Expanding the study to cover cross-cultural analyses may give insight into the wide variety of influences of societal norms and values on adopting and applying technology. Researchers can also work with integrating ethical frameworks with technical evaluations for AI systems with biases against mitigation, reliability, and transparency. Longitudinal studies on the long-term effects of AI and robotics on eldercare outcomes will help policymakers and developers design more inclusive and practical solutions.

8 Conclusion

The deployment of AI and robots as new technologies in elderly care is the path to possibly realizing the rising implications of population aging while at the same time improving the quality of care. This research also emphasizes that AI and robotic systems can support human care by relieving the caregivers of repetitive paperwork, providing suggestions on how to improve their services performance and featuring the roles that social robots and health monitoring systems can play in the emotional support arena. However, the study also brings out some important ethical consideration like privacy, autonomy, attachment, and equity which requires careful consideration in case implementation. From the evaluation of the principles of ethics of autonomy, beneficence, non-malicious intent, and equity the current study articulates a gap between technology and ethical care delivery. Policy makers/the developers are encouraged to create technology that is culturally neutral, free of prejudices and which always honors the dignity of a person. Through creating a collective work among stakeholders and considering the ethical aspect while implementing AI and robotics in eldercare, the elderly will have a new form of care they never experienced before; all these while, human values and equity in society will also be maintained.

Acknowledgments We acknowledge the anonymous reviewers who helped us to frame this manuscript to the next level.

References

Baier, A. (1994). *Moral prejudices: Essays on ethics*. Harvard University Press.

Beard, J. R., Officer, A., de Carvalho, I. A., Sadana, R., Pot, A. M., Michel, J.-P., Lloyd-Sherlock, P., Epping-Jordan, J. E., Peeters, G. M. E. E., Mahanani, W. R., Thiyagarajan, J. A., & Chatterji, S. (2016). The World Report on aging and health: A policy framework for healthy aging. *The Lancet, 387*(10033), 2145–2154. https://doi.org/10.1016/S0140-6736(15)00516-4

Beauchamp, T. L., & Childress, J. F. (1977). *Principles of biomedical ethics*. Oxford University Press.

Beauchamp, T. L., & Rauprich, O. (2016). Principlism. In H. ten Have (Ed.), *Encyclopedia of global bioethics*. Springer. https://doi.org/10.1007/978-3-319-09483-0_348

Brodhead, M. T., Cox, D. J., & Quigley, S. P. (2022). *Practical ethics for effective treatment of autism spectrum disorder: Critical specialties in treating autism and other behavioral challenges* (2nd ed.). Academic Press. https://doi.org/10.1016/C2021-0-02851-1

Calabrò, R. S., Accorinti, M., Porcari, B., Carioti, L., Ciatto, L., Billeri, L., Andronaco, V. A., Galletti, F., Filoni, S., & Naro, A. (2019). Does hand robotic rehabilitation improve motor function by rebalancing interhemispheric connectivity after chronic stroke? Encouraging data from a randomized clinical trial. *Clinical Neurophysiology, 130*(5), 767–780. https://doi.org/10.1016/j.clinph.2019.02.013

Chen, S.-C., Davis, B. H., Kuo, C.-Y., Maclagan, M., Chien, C.-O., & Lin, M.-F. (2022). Can the Paro be my buddy? Meaningful experiences from the perspectives of older adults. *Geriatric Nursing, 43*, 130–137. https://doi.org/10.1016/j.gerinurse.2021.11.011

Cheng, M., & Edwards, D. (2019). A comparative automated content analysis approach on the review of the sharing economy discourse in tourism and hospitality. *Current Issues in Tourism, 22*(1), 35–49.

Dixon, J., Hong, B., & Wu, L. (2021). The robot revolution: Managerial and employment consequences for firms. *Management Science, 67*(9), 5586–5605.

Driver, J. (2011). *Consequentialism* (1st ed.). Routledge. https://doi.org/10.4324/9780203149256

Gao, Q., Prina, M., Wu, Y. T., & Mayston, R. (2022). Unmet healthcare needs among middle-aged and older adults in China. *Age and Ageing, 51*(1), afab235. https://doi.org/10.1093/ageing/afab235

Gerke, S., Minssen, T., & Cohen, G. (2020). Ethical and legal challenges of artificial intelligence-driven healthcare. In E. H. Shortliffe & J. J. Cimino (Eds.), *Artificial intelligence in healthcare* (pp. 295–336). Academic Press. https://doi.org/10.1016/B978-0-12-818438-7.00012-5

Hung, L., Liu, C., Woldum, E., Chaudhury, H., Shankar, K., Fletcher, J., & Van Der Loos, H. M. (2019). The benefits and barriers to using a social robot PARO in care settings: A scoping review. *BMC Geriatrics, 19*(1), 232. https://doi.org/10.1186/s12877-019-1244-6

Kar, A. K., & Dwivedi, Y. K. (2020). Theory building with considerable data-driven research–moving away from the "what" towards the "why". *International Journal of Information Management, 54*, 102205.

Ma, B., Yang, J., Wong, F. K. Y., Wong, A. K. C., Ma, T., Meng, J., Zhao, Y., Wang, Y., & Lu, Q. (2023). Artificial intelligence in elderly healthcare: A scoping review. *Ageing Research Reviews, 83*, 101808. https://doi.org/10.1016/j.arr.2022.101808

Miranda, S., Berente, N., Seidel, S., Safadi, H., & Burton-Jones, A. (2022). Editor's comments: Computationally intensive theory construction: A primer for authors and reviewers. *MIS Quarterly, 46*(2), iii–xviii.

Moyle, W., Jones, C., Sung, B., Bramble, M., O'Dwyer, S., Blumenstein, M., & Estivill-Castro, V. (2016). What effect does an animal robot called CuDDler have on the engagement and emotional response of older people with dementia? A pilot feasibility study. *International Journal of Social Robotics, 8*(1), 145–156. https://doi.org/10.1007/s12369-015-0326-7

Padhan, S., Mohapatra, A., Ramasamy, S. K., & Agrawal, S. (2023). Artificial intelligence (AI) and robotics in elderly healthcare: Enabling independence and quality of life. *Cureus, 15*(8), e42905. https://doi.org/10.7759/cureus.42905

Rabheru, K. (2022). Mental health promotion and risk reduction strategies for mental disorders in older persons: Why should governments and policymakers care? *Consortium Psychiatricum, 3*(1), 22–28.

Roberts, M. E., Stewart, B. M., & Tingley, D. (2019). Stm: An R package for structural topic models. *Journal of Statistical Software, 91*, 1–40.

Sahoo, M., Pragyan, P., Rout, H., & Jakovljevic, M. (2023). Consequences of India's population aging to its healthcare financing and provision. *Journal of Medical Economics, 26*(1), 1–24. https://doi.org/10.1080/13696998.2023.2178164

Sharma, A., Rana, N. P., & Nunkoo, R. (2021). Fifty years of information management research: A conceptual structure analysis using structural topic modeling. *International Journal of Information Management, 58*, 102316.

Timmermann, J. (2013). Kantian dilemmas? Moral conflict in Kant's ethical theory. *Archiv für Geschichte der Philosophie, 95*(1), 36–64. https://doi.org/10.1515/agph-2013-0002

Trujillo, G. M. (2021). *Principlism in biomedical ethics: Respect for autonomy, non-maleficence, beneficence, and justice*. 1000-Word Philosophy. Retrieved December 7, 2024, from https://1000wordphilosophy.com/2021/02/16/principlism-in-biomedical-ethics/#_ftn2

United Nations Population Fund (UNFPA). (2023). *India aging: Elderly to make up 20% of the population by 2050*. UNFPA report. https://india.unfpa.org/en/news/india-ageing-elderly-make-20-population-2050-unfpa-report

Wu, X., & Huo, Y. (2023). Impact of introducing service robots on consumer satisfaction: Empirical evidence from hotels. *Technological Forecasting and Social Change, 194*, 122718. https://doi.org/10.1016/j.techfore.2023.122718

Yadav, J., Yadav, A., Misra, M., Rana, N.P. and Zhou, J. (2023), "Role of social media in technology adoption for sustainable agriculture practices: Evidence from Twitter Analytics", *Communications of the Association for Information Systems, 52*(1), p.35

Youvan, D. (2024). *Transforming elder care: The evolution of rest home care and the future impact of AI and robotics*. https://doi.org/10.13140/RG.2.2.30929.95847.

Zhao, Y., & Li, J. (2024). Opportunities and challenges of integrating artificial intelligence in China's elderly care services. *Scientific Reports, 14*, 9254. https://doi.org/10.1038/s41598-024-60067-w

Zhao, A. P., Li, S., Cao, Z., Hu, P. J.-H., Wang, J., Xiang, Y., Xie, D., & Lu, X. (2024). AI for science: Predicting infectious diseases. *Journal of Safety Science and Resilience, 5*(2), 130–146. https://doi.org/10.1016/j.jnlssr.2024.02.002

Index

A
AI in workplace wellness, 35–37, 46, 49

C
Corporate wellness, 1, 63

D
Disaster management, 54, 60

E
Emotional regulation, 1, 2, 5, 8, 9, 11
Employee well-being, 35–49, 63, 64, 71, 73, 74

F
Farmers, 53–60
Floods, 53–60

H
Health and healing, 1–11
Human resource management, 48

M
Memories, 3, 18, 21, 25, 28, 56, 58, 81
Mental health, 3–5, 16, 23, 36–38, 54–56, 59, 60, 63, 71, 73–75, 84
Mindfulness, 1–11, 15–28, 72, 73
Mindfulness and meditation, 1–11

O
Organizational productivity, 43, 47, 63, 64, 76

P
Psychological distress, 53–60
Psychology, 4, 15

T
Trauma and anxiety, 54, 56

W
Wellbeing, 1–5, 7–11, 15–21, 24, 27, 28, 36, 37, 39, 47–49, 56, 60, 63, 69, 72–76, 78, 79, 81, 84, 85, 88

S. Batra (ed.), *Health and Wellness for All: Navigating Pathways to a Better Life*, Advances in Mental Health and Addiction,
https://doi.org/10.1007/978-3-031-98979-7

MIX
Papier aus verantwortungsvollen Quellen
Paper from responsible sources
FSC® C105338

If you have any concerns about our products,
you can contact us on
ProductSafety@springernature.com

In case Publisher is established outside the EU,
the EU authorized representative is:
Springer Nature Customer Service Center GmbH
Europaplatz 3, 69115 Heidelberg, Germany

Printed by Libri Plureos GmbH
in Hamburg, Germany